NORTH DEVON COUNTRY

IN OLD PHOTOGRAPHS

FROM THE BEAFORD PHOTOGRAPHIC ARCHIVE

PART TWO

A threshing scene c. 1918. Mr G. Hearn owned a threshing business up to 1930. The scene is at Horwood Farm (behind North Devon Meat) and Farmer Stanbury is in the centre of picture with a cane.

NORTH DEVON COUNTRY

IN OLD PHOTOGRAPHS

FROM THE BEAFORD PHOTOGRAPHIC ARCHIVE

PART TWO

COMPILED BY
BERYL YATES

ALAN SUTTON
1989

Alan Sutton Publishing
Gloucester

First published 1989

British Library Cataloguing in Publication Data

North Devon Country in old photographs.
1. Devon, North Devon, history
I. Beaford Centre
942.3'352

ISBN 0–86299–727–5

DEDICATION

I would like to dedicate this third book to my five children – John, Jane, Michael and David Yates, and Amanda Rendle.

Typesetting and origination by
Alan Sutton Publishing
Printed in Great Britain by
WBC Print Limited

CONTENTS

INTRODUCTION

I came across my first old photographs of Devon at an 'Oldest Photo' competition run by Dolton Women's Institute 15 years ago. At the suggestion of John Lane, the founding director of the Beaford Centre, I had already begun to make a photographic record of modern-day life in North Devon. But now the quality of the old photographs submitted for this competition – in one smallish village alone – and the interest they generated, prompted the idea that I should also search out and copy old photographs throughout the same area, to make a second, parallel, record of local life as it was around the turn of the century.

I began by borrowing those competition entries. Talking to their owners released a flood of local history. 'That's my grandfather. He was a postman. Twelve miles a day his round used to be – all on foot, winter and summer.' 'That was the first car in the village.' 'That's where they used to have the market twice a week. I can mind that street full of cattle, wall to wall.' The details poured out: potted biographies, funny anecdotes, old farming techniques and wistful reminiscences of a vanished way of life.

As I juggled frantically with the copying equipment and my scribbled index cards, other packages would appear, whole albums, even shoeboxes, bulging with more and more material.

One owner would pass me on to another. This one would have an anonymous group. Her aunt in another village would know the names of every single face. 'Oh! that's so-and-so. I went to school with him.'

Other Women's Institutes got wind of the scheme and contacted me. They asked for slide shows of what I had already, and the enthusiastic audiences would produce as much again. Sometimes the primary schools brought me collections. Often I would be photographing some present-day scene, and a casual reference to the past would bring out the albums again.

Luckily for the Archive, Devonians cherish their past. From their forebears in the 1900s, who bought these early photographs direct from the local photographer, to the modern owners who can't bear to throw them away, they have valued them as 'a little bit of history': amazing, touching, even comic, but above all, precious as proof of how things were. It is hardly surprising that they do. The changes in population, transport, communications, farming methods, costume, the look of the place, and the whole outlook on life, which have occurred in North Devon since these photographs were taken are simply staggering. The children who stared at the camera in those solemn rows in the early 1900s probably walked two miles to school in hand-me-down clothes, with a baked potato in their pockets for their midday meal. At school they sat in rigid rows, chanting lists of facts, and practising laborious copper-plate script. Afterwards they went home to a candle-lit, two-bedroomed, tied cottage housing a family of eight or ten. They lived on bread and bacon and home-grown vegetables. They curtseyed and touched their caps to the Squire, and went to church at least once every Sunday. When needed, they stayed home from school, and went to work in the fields along with the men, potato-picking, bird-scaring and leading the harvest waggons. At thirteen, they left school for good to be live-in farm boys and dairy-maids. The biggest events of their year were probably the Sunday school charabanc outing to the sea, and the annual carnival or fair. Otherwise, they made their own entertainment. Exeter, some thirty miles away, was the outer limit of their world.

Now, a mere eighty years on, within one lifetime even, the people of North Devon have lived through two world wars, Depression, the setting up of the Welfare State, the European Community, the conquest of space. Some of those same children now have cars, tractors, combine harvesters, washing-machines and microwave ovens. Their smart new houses are dominated by the television set; their villages are full of strangers; and their churches half-empty. They can fly to America to visit relations; holiday on the Costa Brava; buy huge machines with grants and loans; and get new hips and hearts on the National Health. No wonder the simple, orderly, self-reliant life the old pictures portray seems light years away.

But would one, given the chance, return to those far-off days recalled with such nostalgia? For the leisurely pace of life, perhaps. And for the comradeship of the old communities, where everyone knew everyone else from the cradle to the grave, and farmwork, however hard, was a sociable trade.

For me, the greatest lure is in the buildings themselves as these photographs show them, with their simple but satisfying shapes and harmonious proportions, built of local materials, and blending into their landscape as if they were part of it. Few sharp concrete edges or factory-made slates and frames had yet come to whip them into line. Nor had the road become the broad slash of tarmac that knifes its way through the modern village, now that the demands of traffic take precedence over all else. In the old pictures the road is part of the countryside; and the houses seem to grow out of it naturally.

One should pay tribute here to the early photographers, who lugged their cumbersome wooden cameras, tripods, black cloths and glass negatives so far afield. They were professionals, albeit part-time, for most of them were also the village shop-keeper, chemist, dentist or vet. The day was still to come when every family would take its 'snaps' with its own Box Brownie. These early photographs were well composed and printed with care. Many of them have a quiet elegance. Of course such a process was better adapted to street scenes and posed groups than action shots, and, sadly, interiors were technically very difficult. I am always especially pleased when another good interior turns up.

As the flood of old photographs grew, so the task of copying, indexing and printing reference prints became more and more time-consuming. For five years I was lucky enough to have George Tucker, a local photographer, to help extensively with this work. Finally, in 1987, Beryl Yates was appointed curator, and the old photographs were placed, thankfully, in her capable hands. Since then, she and her changing band of part-time helpers have spent two strenuous years sorting, cross-referencing, printing, exhibiting and marketing the collection (which now numbers over 7,500 negatives, and is still growing).

Together, the old photographs and my own modern record, called collectively the Beaford Archive, form one of the largest rural photographic collections in the country, and are soon to have a permanent home in renovated barns adjoining the Beaford Centre. Here, it is hoped, we shall at last have room to expand, with adequate storage and retrieval systems, darkroom and study facilities, changing exhibitions, and a shop to sell prints, books, postcards, etc., relating to the collections.

The present pair of volumes compiled by Beryl Yates is only a part of what the Beaford Archive has to offer. She has selected the pictures in them primarily to meet the demand of local people for a record of their own particular patch – as it was in their childhood, perhaps, or in their parents' and grandparents' day. The photographs are grouped village by village, and Beryl has introduced each group with a short extract from Kelly's Directory for 1902 in order to give some background information on each community at around the time when the pictures were taken.

I am sure these books will give a great deal of pleasure and interest to both native Devonians and the wider public who love this countryside.

James Ravilious
The Beaford Centre

GOODLEIGH is a parish and village, on the river Yeo, which bounds the parish on the northern side and flows into the Taw; 3 miles east-by-north from Barnstaple station on the Torrington branch of the London and South Western railway and 1½ south from Chelfham station on the Lynton and Barnstaple railway, in the North Western division of the county, Braunton hundred and petty sessional division, Barnstaple union and county court district, rural deanery of Sherwill, archdeaconry of Barnstaple and diocese of Exeter. The church of St. Gregory is an edifice of stone in the Perpendicular style, consisting of chancel, nave, south aisle, south porch and an embattled western tower, with pinnacles, containing 6 bells, dating from 1743 to 1828: there are two monuments to the Acland family, d. 1633-55: the east window is stained: the church was rebuilt in 1881-2, at a cost of about

A view of the village.

£2,500, and will seat 181 persons. The register dates from the year 1538. The living is a rectory, net yearly value £160, and 35 acres of glebe, with residence, in the gift of Edward Bourchier Savile esq. of Okehampton, and held since 1880 by the Rev. Frederick Jarratt, of King's College, London. Here are Congregational and Bible Christian chapels. Acland's charity amounts to 26s. Gage Hodge esq. of Pounds, near Plymouth, is the principal landowner. The soil is loamy; the subsoil, gravelly. The chief crops are wheat, oats and barley. The area is 1,162 acres; rateable value, £1,595; the population in 1901 was 253.

NORTHLEIGH is a hamlet, ¾ mile north.

Sexton, John Bowden.

Post Office.—John Parish, sub-postmaster. Letters through Barnstaple arrive by train to Chelfham station at 7.5 a.m.; dispatched at 6.30 p.m. Postal orders are issued here, but not paid. The nearest money order & telegraph office is at Barnstaple, 3 miles distant Letter Boxes—Gunn, cleared at 5.35 p.m.; Snapper, 5.45 p.m.; Westacott, 5.5 p.m.; Waytown, 5.20 p.m

National School (mixed), built in 1875, for 60 children; average attendance, 45; Miss Frances Boon, mistress

Dudley Miss, 2 Barbara villas
Jarratt Rev. Frederick, Rectory
Plaister George, Northleigh butts
Rook John, Northleigh cottage
Stoneman Frederick, Snapper
Willink Miss, Yeotown

COMMERCIAL.

Barmam George, farmer, Ballers
Blackwell Fredk. basket mkr. Snappr
Crook George, shopkeeper
Davie John, farmer, Northleigh

Fry James, farmer, Cross
Furze William, farmer, Northleigh
Gill Wm. Hedley, frmr. Northleigh
Guard George, farmer, Snapper
Hill John, farmer, Chelfham mill
Hopper Thomas, blacksmith
Isaac John, farmer, Great Lilly
Joslin Frederick, farmer, Eastacott
Keirle John Walter, farmer, Coombe
Lewis James, farmer, The Hall farm
Mugford George B. farmr. Snapper
Norman Mary (Mrs.), dairy

Parish John, post office
Prideaux Jn. market grdnr. Rectory
Richards Jn. shoe ma. & assist.oversr
Ridd James, carpenter
Shapland Jane (Mrs.), New inn
Stanbury James,farmer, Yeotown,Lilly & Ivy lodge
Tucker Jn. farmr. Conisbeer,Snapper
Tucker James, farmer, Northleigh
Watts Hy. butcher & farmer,Crow hill
Watts Joseph,farmer & seedsman,Dean

The village, showing the New Inn pub.

LANDKEY is a village and parish on a tributary of the river Taw, 2½ miles east-south-east from Barnstaple stations on the London and South Western and Great Western railways, in the North Western division of the county, South Molton hundred, Braunton petty sessional division, Barnstaple union and county district, rural deanery of Sherwill, archdeaconry of Barnstaple and diocese of Exeter. The church of St. Paul is a building of stone in the Perpendicular style, consisting of chancel, nave, north aisle, north and south chapels, south porch and an embattled western tower containing a clock and 6 bells, all cast in 1788 from a previous peal of four: in the church are recumbent effigies in stone of the 12th or 13th centuries, discovered during the restoration of the church in 1870; one having been built up in the wall where it was placed, and the other two concealed beneath the pews; two of these are figures of ladies, in wimples and flowing dresses, one wearing a long mantle; the other effigy is that of a cross-legged knight; they are conjectured to represent members of the Acland or Beaupell families, both which had possessions here; there is also a monument with life-size figures to Sir Arthur Acland, ob. 1610, and Elynor, his wife, ob. 1645: in the south chapel is a stained window and a hagioscope; the east window and one in the nave are also stained: the font is octagonal and probably of the 15th century: there are 204 sittings. The register dates from the year 1602. The living is a vicarage, net yearly value £310, including 35 acres of glebe, with residence, in the gift of the Bishop of Exeter, and held since 1901 by the Rev. James Furneaux Powning M.A. of Cambridge University. Here is a Wesleyan chapel, built in 1862, and one for Bible Christians, built in 1865. There are charities of about £110 yearly value. Willesleigh, the property of William Gage Hodge esq. is now the residence of Lady Clark. Acland Barton, now a farmhouse, is the property of Sir Charles T. D. Acland bart. and was the original seat of his family. The Hon. Mark G. K. Rolle is lord of the manor, once held by the Dennys. Sir C. T. D. Acland bart. the Duke of Bedford, T. J. Dennis esq. Henry Law esq. William Gage Hodge esq. of Glazebrook House, South Brent. William Thorne Buckingham esq. and Albert Edward Kemp Thorne esq. of Penzance are the principal landowners. The soil is loamy; subsoil, clay. The chief crops are wheat, oats and barley. The area is 3,183 acres; assessable value, £2,943; the population in 1901 was 621.

Parish Clerk, Edward Buckingham.

Post, M. O. & T. O., T. M. O., Express Delivery, Parcel Post, S. B. & Annuity & Insurance Office.—George Hill, sub-postmaster. Letters from Barnstaple by mail cart, arriving at 7.10 a.m. & returning at 6.30 p.m

Letter Boxes.—Landkeytown, cleared at 6.15 p.m. & Swymbridge, Newland, cleared at 6.20 p.m

Schools.

Church (mixed), built in 1870, for about 100 children: average attendance, 50; Clement Richards, master

Wesleyan, built in 1862 & enlarged in 1872, for 150 children; average attendance, 114; Edward Searson Slack, master

Landkey – a view from the east.

Clark Lady, Willesleigh
Crang William John, Ferncott
Powning Rev. James Furneaux M.A. (vicar), Vicarage
Thomas Arthur L. Prospect house

COMMERCIAL.

Adams William, beer retailer
Alford John, yeoman, Dean
Andrew William, farmer, Whiddon
Arthur Geo. farmer, Lower Babeleigh
Bale Samuel, nurseryman, Westacott
Bryant Philip, farmr. East Sth. Hays
Bryant Henry, grocer
Buckingham William Thorne, yeoman, Plymshurst
Clements William, farmer, Hill
Darch John, miller (water), Landkey mls
Dennis Wm. butcher, Newland mills
Dunn Josiah, farmer, Hunnacott
Elliott Robert, road contractor
Gamon George, seed merchant & insurance agent & maltster
Gould John, blacksmith, Landkeytown
Hancock Jas. farmer, Harford Barton
Hill Geo. & Son, blcksmths. Post off
Hoad William E. C. boot & shoe air
Jones Edward Staddon, yeoman, assistant overseer & assessor, Hammetts
Jones Wm. miller (water), Castle mill
Lewis James, farmer, Hall
Petherick Robert, farmer, Ackland Bartn
Rew William, grocer & miller
Southwood John, farmer, builder & contractor, South Hayse
Stanbury Mary Ann (Mrs.), farmer, Westacott
Stanbury William, farmer, Yoalden
Symonds John, farmer, Hunnacott

The village — west end.

Taylor Elizabeth (Mrs.), Ring of Bells P.H. & maltster
Watts Mathew, farmer, Hill
Tucker John & Son, farmers, Bradninch
Webber Ann (Mrs.), farmer, Portmore
Webber John, farmer, Pill
Wybron Ernest, farmer, Prospect

The petrol filling station and Mrs Gould's shop.

The War Memorial.

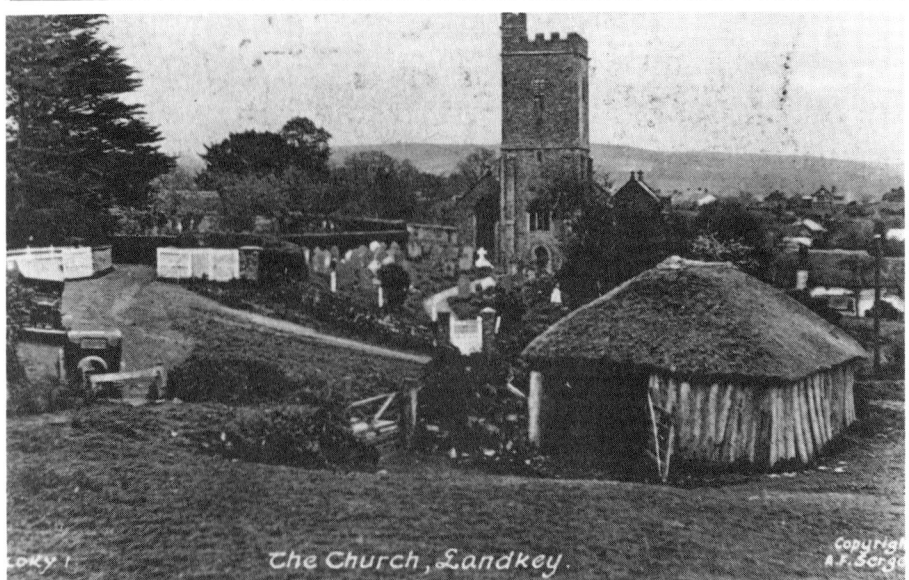

The Church, Landkey.

The Ring o' Bells, the church and the church cottage.

A courtyard scene. Can any reader supply the name of the location please?

An unknown lady, Landkey. She has such a beautiful cape, intricate hat, and beadwork embroidery on her cuffs. I wish I knew her name.

From the sublime to the ridiculous! Bill King talking to his pig.

The family at Portmore. In Kelly Mrs Ann Webber is listed as farmer of Portmore.

John Darch Jnr. with his penny-farthing bicycle.

LANGTREE is a parish and village, 4 miles south-west from Torrington station of a branch of the North Devon line of the London and South Western railway, and 9 south from Bideford, in the Northern division of the county, Shebbear hundred, Torrington petty sessional division, union and county court district, and in the rural deanery of Torrington, archdeaconry of Barnstaple and diocese of Exeter. The church (dedication unknown) is an ancient building of stone in the Perpendicular style, consisting of chancel, nave, north aisle, south porch and an embattled western tower, 60 feet in height and containing 6 bells; the first three and the fifth date from 1816, the fourth, cast in 1835, and new third and treble, cast in 1879 at a cost of £80, are all by Taylor, of Oxford; weight of tenor 11 cwt.: there is a memorial window in the north aisle, erected in 1873, to the Rev. John Guard, a former rector of this parish; two other windows inserted by him in memory of his wife and daughter, and a memorial window placed in 1891 to the Ven. Archdeacon Barnes, 17 years rector of this parish (1873-90): the organ was erected in 1891: there are 250 sittings. The register dates from the year 1659. The living is a rectory, net yearly value £310, with residence and 72 acres of glebe, in the gift of the Hon. Mark G. K. Rolle, and held since 1890 by the Rev. Edward John Hall M.A. of Caius College, Cambridge. There are two chapels for Bible Christians. The charities are of about £45 yearly value. The Hon. Mark George Kerr Rolle, who is lord of the manor, the Rev. Hubert G. de C.

Stevens-Guille M.A. of Little Torrington, and John Elias Tucker esq. are the chief landowners. Clements Week belongs to John Tanton Copp esq. Berry and Week are the property of Mr. John Webber. Chapmans belongs to Miss C. Penhale; Withicott to Mr. H. Ley. Miss Dayman, of East Putford, Mr. William Henry Hackwill, Mr. Leonard Risdleigh, Mr. Edwin Brookes, and Mr. Samuel Henry Deyman are also landowners. The Tucker family have held land here since the reign of Charles II. The soil is clayey; subsoil, clay and stone. The chief crops are wheat and oats. The area is 4,741 acres; rateable value, £2,893; the population in 1891 was 672 in the ecclesiastical parish, and 612 in the civil parish in 1901.

By Local Government Board Order, 14,971, Alscott was transferred to Peters Marland, and by Order, 14,970, Muffery was added to this parish from Frithelstock, March 24, 1884, for civil purposes.

Parish Clerk, John Mills.

Post Office.—William Trigger, sub-postmaster. Letters through Torrington, received at 10 a.m. & dispatched at 4.30 p.m. Postal orders are issued here, but not paid. Torrington is the nearest money order & telegraph office, 4 miles distant

Wall Letter Boxes.—Stibb Cross, cleared at 3 p.m. week days only; Berry Cross, 4 p.m. week days only; Week, 5.5 p.m. week days only

Parochial School (mixed), built in 1840, for 136 children; average attendance, 88; Arthur Austerberry, master; Miss Mary Ann Huxtable, infants' mistress

The Green Dragon public house, c. 1911.

The main street, Langtree.

Hall Rev. Edward John M.A. Rectory
Whitlock Miss, Rose cottage
COMMERCIAL.
Andrews Philip, farmer, West Browns
Ayre John, shoe maker, Berry cross
Bale William, tailor
Balkwill James, farmer, Lambert
Balsdon Thomas, farmer, Muffery
Blight John, blacksmith, Stibb Cross
Blight Wm. shopkeeper, Stibb Cross
Bromell John, Union inn, Stibb Cross
Brooks Edwin, yeoman, Hillashmoor
Brooks Ann (Mrs.), farmer, Ashbury
Burrows William, carpenter
Cole Philip, farmer, Langtree Week
Copp John Tanton, farmer & land-
owner, Clements Week
Copp Willie Shamburgh, miller(water),
Higher mill
Curtice John, farmer, Cholash & West
Ashbury
Davey William, shoe maker
Ellis William, farmer, Stibb farm

Fishleigh Leonard, yeoman, Stibb Cross
Furse Samuel, farmer, Burston
Goss William, farmer, Stowford & Buda
Gribble Henry, Green Dragon P.H
Guscott Jn. farmer, Higher Stowford
Guscott Sl. J. farmer, Lower Collacott
Hackwill Wm. Hy. farmer, Suddon
Holman Elias, machinist & agricul-
tural implement agent, Week
Horn Samuel, tailor &c. Stibb Cross
Hutchings Thomas, farmer, Earlswd
Huxtable Mary Ann (Mrs.), farmer,
Withacott
Huxtable Richard, farmer, Birchill &
Smallbridge
Jones Philip, farmer, Lower Water-
town & Bearehouse
Kallaway William, farmer, Little Com-
fort & Lower mill
Ley Charles, farmer, Withacott
Lockyer Elizabeth (Mrs.), machinists
Martin James, shoe maker
Martin Wm. Henry, farmer, Putshole

Moore John, farmer, East Brown's
Netherway Henry, farmer, Dogaport
Nicholls Thos. frmr. & butchr. Wedlnds
Pellew John, farmer, Birchill cottage
Pellew John, jun. farmer, Gortlease
Pope James, farmer, Thatton
Pope Thomas, farmer, Higher Thorn
Sanders John, carpenter & wheel-
wright, Stibb Cross
Sanders Samuel John, assistant over-
seer & clerk to the Parish Council
Sanders Stephen, carpenter & paper-
hanger &c. Sandy lane
Short Thomas, mason & farmer
Short William, mason
Thorne Richard, blacksmith
Thorne William, blacksmith, Lake
Trewin Thomas, farmer, Collacott
Trigger Wm. grocer&draper, Post office
Tucker John Elias, yeoman, Rivaton
Vanstone Wm. carpntr.& wheelwright
Walters William, farmer
Webber John, yeoman, Berry

The church interior.

The Rectory.

Stibb Cross, the blacksmith's shop.

MARIANSLEIGH is a parish and village seated on a hill overlooking the valley of the Mole, 4 miles south-east from South Molton station, on the Great Western railway, in the Northern division of the county,

ALSWERE, 1¼ miles south, and LITTLE SILVER, 1¼ south-west, are hamlets.

Nellie and Herbert Mildon in their wedding car, c. 1910. With them was Mrs Partridge (née Cook), a widow. The photo was taken at Little Silver where the couple lived and continued Mr Partridge's business (tobacconist and poultry and egg dealer). They despatched their goods from South Molton railway station, and brought back coal as ordered.

(Letters for Alswere are delivered direct from South Molton.)
Adams William, Alswere
Snell John Carpenter, Alswere
Winnifrith Rev. Alfred M.A. Rectory
COMMERCIAL.
Ayre Henry, farmer, Trittencott
Ayre William, farmer, Milltown
Bennett George, farmer, Rowcleave
Clogg Elizabeth (Mrs.), miller (water), Alswere mills
Crook Samuel, farmer
Cooke William, butter, poultry & game dealer & corn mer. Lit. Silver

Curtis Frank, cowkeeper, Nutcleave
Eastmond James, farmer, New house
Fewings William, farmer, Westacott
Hill John, farmer, Spenscott
Hodge Peter, carpenter
Holmes Robert, farmer, Little Silver
Kerslake Jesse, blacksmith, grocer & corn dealer, Alswere
Kingdon James, Butchers' Arms P.H. Alswere
Kingdon William, White Hart P.H. & farmer, Alswere
Lee Robert, shoe maker, Alswere
Mildon Wm. frmr. Mariansleigh Barton

Setherton John, farmer, Greencap
Shapland Francis, farmer, Buthay
Shapland Walter, farmer, Upcott
Smith Richard, farmer, Tidlake
Smyth William John, farmer & asst. overseer, assessor & collector of taxes & agent to Atlas Insurance Co. Hobby house, Alswere
Tidball Harriet(Mrs.), shopkpr.& dairy
Tucker Jn. Inkerman, farmer, Eastacot
Tucker Samuel, King's Arms P.H. & farmer
Warren Thos. farmer & butcher, Yeo
Webber Robert, farmer, Hilltown

General view, c. 1904. In the foreground, from left to right: George Heywood and his three sisters, Fred Clements, -?- Meardon, -?- Madge and his sister (with hat), Bill Clements, Bill Chudleigh. The man in the background is Philip Madge. The boy by the shutter on the right is Henry Richards.

MEETH is a scattered parish and village on the river Torridge, 10 miles west-by-south from Eggesford station on the North Devon branch of the London and South Western railway, 3 north from Hatherleigh and 10 north from Okehampton, in the Western division of the county, Shebbear hundred, Hatherleigh petty sessional division, Okehampton union and county court district, rural deanery of Torrington, archdeaconry of Barnstaple and diocese of Exeter. A fine stone bridge of 3 arches crosses the Torridge at the southern boundary of the parish. The church of St. Michael is an ancient edifice of stone of mixed styles, consisting of chancel, nave, south porch and an embattled western tower with pinnacles, containing 4 bells: in the church is a monument to John Lempriere D.D. of Pembroke College, Oxford, author of the well-known Classical Dictionary, and head master of Abingdon school from 1792 to 1810; he was rector of this parish from 1811 and died in London 1st February, 1824; there is also a monument, erected in 1848, to the late Mrs. Lamb, with a group in marble representing the assumption of the deceased: the church was thoroughly renovated in 1893, the pews being lowered and replaced, the chancel lengthened and a vestry added: there are 84 sittings. The register dates from the year 1653. The living is a rectory, net yearly value £189, with residence and 25 acres of glebe, in the gift of the Rev. Hubert George de Carteret Stevens Guille M.A. of Churchford, and held since 1886 by the Rev. John Henry Kempe. The Bible Christian chapel at Giffords Hill, erected in 1870, will seat 120 persons. There are charities of £3 yearly value, left by a Mr. Germain, out of which the rector has 10s. for preaching a sermon; and there is also a sum of 5s. yearly left by Mrs. Germain. Robert J. Preston-Whyte esq. of Leigh House, Chulmleigh, who is lord of the manor, Lord Clinton and Hugh Acland esq. of Bow R.S.O. are the chief landowners The soil is dunland; the subsoil is clay. The chief crops are barley, wheat, oats and roots. The area is 2,559 acres of land and 23 of water; rateable value, £1,594; the population in 1901 was 209.

Sexton, Robert Meardon.

Post Office.—William Clements, sub-postmaster. Letters are received through Hatherleigh R.S.O. arrive at 7.30 a.m.; dispatched at 5.40 p.m. Postal orders are issued here, but not paid. The nearest money order & telegraph office is at Hatherleigh, 3 miles distant

Church School (mixed), founded in 1874, for 60 children; average attendance, 31; Mrs. Mary Jane Battishill, mistress

The village street. (See opposite page for a close up of this group of children.)

An unknown family group.

Edgeworth John, Alma cottage
Kempe Rev. John Henry, Rectory
Battishill George, shoe maker
Blackmore John, farmer, Stone Cross
Clements Wm. shopkpr. & post office
Cobbledick James & Sons, farmers, Friar's hele
Cobbledick Lewis, farmer, Stockleigh

Cockwill Shadrack, machinist & crptnr
Heale Caleb, farmer, Great Borna
Heywood Geo. Hy.frmr. Western town
Hooper John, farmer, Woolladon
Hurford Elizabeth (Mrs.) & Son, farmers, Eastern town
King William, farmer, Stockhay
Meardon William, shoe maker

Millman Philip, farmer, Park
Murrin John, farmer, Gifford's hele
Page William, woodman to R. J. Preston-White esq. J.P
Quick Stephen George, farmer, Crockers hill
Spicer John, New inn
Westaway William, tailor

A cottage interior.

MERTON is a parish and village, on the river Torridge, 7 miles south-east from Torrington terminal station of a branch of the London and South Western railway, in the Northern division of the county, Shebbear hundred, Torrington petty sessional division, union and county court district, and in the rural deanery of Torrington, archdeaconry of Barnstaple and diocese of Exeter. The church of **All Saints** is an edifice of stone in the Perpendicular style, consisting of chancel, nave, north aisle, south transept, south porch and an embattled western tower, with pinnacles, containing 6 bells, of which the fourth dates from 1669, the tenor from 1752; the first and fifth were cast by Warner, of London, in 1858; the second is inscribed "Plebs omnis plaudit ut me tam sæpius audit"; weight of tenor 10 cwt.: the church retains an ancient register chest, and has five stained windows, one of which is a memorial: the north-east window, a work of early date, was restored and filled with stained glass in 1847: in the north aisle is a memorial window to the rector's daughter: the church was restored in 1875 at a cost of £1,951, under the direction of Mr. R. Medley Fulford, architect, the Speccott aisle being rebuilt at the cost of J. C. Moore-Stevens esq. the chancel by the late rector, and the remainder of the church by Lord Clinton and others; the screens and fittings being the work of Hems, of Exeter: in 1895 a new organ, the gift of parishioners and friends, was erected as a memorial to the late Rev. James Cory Kempe M.A. for over 40 years rector of this parish: there are 310 sittings. In 1892 a lych gate was erected at the eastern entrance to the church. The register of baptisms and burials dates from the year 1687; marriages, 1688. The living is a rectory, net yearly value £273, with residence and 63 acres of glebe, in the gift of Lord Clinton, and held

High Street.

since 1895 by the Rev. Frederic Robinson M.A. of Wadham College, Oxford, hon. chaplain to Sir Massey Lopes bart. Here is a Bible Christian chapel. There are charities of 5s. yearly value, left in 1727 by Thomas Langdon, who also left £1 for the rector for preaching a sermon on the anniversary of his death, Sept. 5th. Here is an Industrial Home for 25 orphan girls, supported by Lady Clinton. The Victoria saw mill, erected in 1887, is driven by water-power from a large ornamental lake of 3 acres, the property of Lord Clinton. Lord Clinton, Lord-Lieut. of the county, is lord of the manor and owner of the whole parish, with the exception of Great Potheridge, which belongs to the Hon. Mark George Kerr Rolle, and Speccott, which is the property of John Curzon Moore-Stevens esq. of Winscott. The soil is dun; subsoil, clay. The chief crops are wheat, oats and barley. The area is 4,046 acres of land and 43 of water; rateable value, £2,937; the population in 1901 was 507.

GREAT POTHERIDGE was the birthplace (December 6th, 1608) of General Monk, afterwards Duke of Albemarle, who is said to have been baptised at Landcross, near Bideford. He died January 3rd, 1670, and was buried in Westminster Abbey.

Parish Clerk, Thomas Bealey.

Post, M. O. & T. O., T. M. O., Express Delivery, Parcel Post, S. B. & Annuity & Insurance Office.—Thomas Bright, sub-postmaster. Letters received through Dolton R.S.O. North Devon, about 7.25 a.m.; dispatched at about 5.50 p.m

National School (mixed), for 140 children; average attendance, 82; Francis Henry Hugo Cresswell, master

The Malt Scoop Inn with a 'growler' coach in front.

Ford Mrs. Oxenham court
Houlditch Edward H. Bounsalls
Robinson Rev. Frederic M.A. Rectory

COMMERCIAL.

Andrews John, farmer, Gt. Potheridge
Ball James, farmer, Speccott
Bonnifant Frederick H. farmer, Little Potheridge
Brook James & Edwin, farmers, Pink hill
Burrow Richard, farmer, Downs
Ching Richard, farmer, Newberry
Cudmore Henry, boot & shoe maker
Cudmore Richard, boot & shoe maker

Eames Alfred, head gardener to Lord Clinton, Gardener's cottage
Elliott Joseph, sewing machine agent
Fairchild John B. farmer, Dunsbear
Ford James, farmer, Yondermere
Heale John, farmer, Great wood
Industrial Orphan Home(Miss Lownes, matron)
Isaacs John, farmer, Ball's farm
Knight Alfred, miller (water), Merton mill
Merton Cash Stores (W. A. Symons, manager)
Moore William, farmer, Yeory
Newcombe Jane (Mrs.), farmer, Ford

Norman Henry, farmer, Colehouse
Petheric Thomas, farmer, Merton Mill farm
Quance John Robert, farmer, Towell
Quance Samuel, blacksmith
Sanders Wm. wheelwright & carpenter
Snell Thomas, farmer, Moor hills
Stacey Wm. Thos. frmr. Rumbledwn
Trick Thomas, blacksmith
Trickey Messrs. farmers, Grange
Trott James, Malt Scoop P.H
Waldron William, farmer, Norton
Wright Henry, clerk of works to Lord Clinton's estates, Rose hill

A view of the main road and the shop. Mr Elliot's studio is the far house.

Shepherds Court. Dr Bickford's surgery is the nearest door and Roy Denford is on the horse.

Mr Joe Elliot, photographer.

Bouncells.

Merton Sawmills.

The Stores.

Meshaw Church.

MESHAW is a parish and village near the road from South Molton to Crediton, 6 miles south-east from the South Molton station on the Devon and Somerset branch of the Great Western railway, 9 from Eggesford station, on the North Devon branch of the London and South Western railway, 7½ north-east from Chulmleigh, 14 north-north-west from Crediton and 15 north-west from Tiverton, in the Northern division of the county, Witheridge hundred, South Molton petty sessional division, union and county court district, and in the rural deanery of South Molton, archdeaconry of Barnstaple and diocese of Exeter. The church of St. John the Baptist, rebuilt in 1838, is an edifice of stone in the Early English style, consisting of chancel, nave, south porch and an embattled western tower containing 4 bells: in the church is a monument to James Courtenay esq. (dated 1683), in memory of whom the tower was rebuilt in 1691: the chancel has been enlarged and a stained east window inserted as a memorial to the Rev. William Heberden Karslake, rector from 1832, and prebendary of Exeter: the west window is a memorial to Mrs. W. H. Karslake: the porch was built and the bells rehung at the expense of the late Miss Preston, lady of the manor, in 1879, and the church was restored during the period 1878-84, at a cost of £742: there are 180 sittings. The register dates from the year 1581. The living is a rectory, net yearly value £191, including 192 acres of glebe, with residence, in the gift of Sir William W. Karslake K.C. of 8, Curzon street, London W, and held since 1891 by the Rev. Alexander Frederick de Gex, who is also rector of Creacombe. Here is a Bible Christian chapel. Robert James Preston-Whyte esq. of Leigh House, Chulmleigh, is lord of the manor and principal landowner. The soil and subsoil vary considerably; on the south side of the parish and a strip on the north-east, Devonshire clay of poor character; through the centre of the parish runs a vein of rich red loam. The chief crops are wheat, barley and roots. The area is 2,095 acres; rateable value, £1,181; the population in 1901 was 198.

Irishcombe, formerly a detached part of the parish of Lapford, and adjoining Meshaw on the east, is now, under the provisions of the Divided Parishes Act, 1882, by Local Government Board Order 16,345, joined to this parish for civil purposes.

Sexton, John Moore.

Post Office.—Frederick Nicholls, sub-postmaster. Letters through South Molton arrive at 9.5 a.m.; letters leave at 4.30 p.m. Postal orders are issued here, but not paid. Bishop's Nymton is the nearest money order & telegraph office, 3½ miles distant

National School (mixed), built in 1875, for 60 children; average attendance, 37; Mrs. Amy Elizabeth Headon, mistress

Meshaw village.

The school group, c. 1898.

de Gex Rev. Alexander Frdk. Rectory

COMMERCIAL.

Adams Henry Kemp, farmer & land-owner, North Downs
Arnold Reuben, frmr. & miller (water)
Bird John, farmer, Bourne bridge
Bird William, farmer, Batteney
Cockram John, thatcher
Cole William, farmer, White stone
Crabb Charles, farmer, Bourne bridge
Crocombe Rd.frmr. North White stone

Elston Jn. farmer, Low. Irishcombe
Grattan Richard, farmer, Narracott
Headon Frederick, farmer, Southall
Headon Richard, poulterer
Holt John, farmer, Blacklands
Hooper Henry John, Gidley Arms P.H. & farmer
Lake John Cooke, farmer, Broadmoor; res. Rull, East Worlington
Ley John, shopkeeper
Ley William, carpenter
Mills James, farmer, Irishcombe

Moore John, blacksmith & sexton
Nicholls Frederick, tailor, Post office
Nott William, farmer, Prescott & Parsonage farms
Pike John, farmer, Moor tenement (res. Romansleigh)
Reed Thomas, farmer, South Down
Squires William, farmer, Broadmoor
Warren Thomas, farmer, Yonderlake
Webber William & George, farmers, Meshaw Barton

34

The village pump, with gas light behind – can anyone name these people please?

Carpenter's shop, and John Ley's general store, the blacksmith's shop was opposite, c. 1909.

Southall Farm.

Two men painting a finished wagon outside Ley's workshop.

The Monkleigh Tiger's Football Team, c. 1907/8. (Some names would be appreciated, please)

MONKLEIGH is a parish and village on the high road from Bideford to Holsworthy, 2 miles north-west from Torrington terminal station of a branch of the London and South Western railway, and 4 south from Bideford, in the North Western division of the county, Shebbear hundred, Bideford petty sessional division, union and county court district, rural deanery of Hartland, archdeaconry of Barnstaple and diocese of Exeter. The church of St. George is an ancient building of stone of Perpendicular character, restored in 1862, and consists of chancel, nave, south aisle, south porch, and an embattled western tower 70 feet in height, containing 6 bells, dated (2) 1711; tenor, 1734; (1) 1771; and (4) 1833; the third is inscribed in Old English characters:— " Misteriis sacris repleat nos d'ca Johannis;" weight of tenor 9 cwt. ; in the Annery (or south) aisle is a canopied altar-tomb with a cusped arch and rich cornice; the upper slab bears matrices of brasses supposed to commemorate Sir William Hankford K.B. Chief Justice of the King's Bench from 1414 to 1422 : in the north wall of the chancel is a brass effigy of a man in armour kneeling, formerly placed on a high tomb, now removed, and commemorating James Coffin esq. ob. Dec. 15, 1566: on a flat stone in the south aisle is a brass scroll, held by two angels, with inscription to Jas. Seyntleger esq. ob.

Feb. 8, 1509, and below a shield with St. Ledger impaling Boteler: some of the windows are stained : the Annery aisle also contains some finely-carved bench ends and portions of screen work of the 16th century, displaying the arms of St. Ledger, Butler Rochford, Hankford, Stapledon, Knyvett, Clifton and other families, as well as the emblems of the Passion and various heraldic badges; some new parclose screens have been erected : in the north or Venton aisle is a monument of marble, with effigies incised on slate of a man and his two wives kneeling facing each other at a desk, and behind them 6 children, and below an inscription to Henry Harding esq. of Long Breedy, Dorset, bur. Feb. 28, 1627, Gertrude (Bamfylde) his first wife, and Eliza (Snowe) his second wife : (Coffyn) wife of Hugh Prust, gent. and her infant, ob. 1646: near this is a monument with demi-effigies to William Gaye, of Hedd, ob. 1651, and Elizabeth (Coffyn) his wife: there are 200 sittings : in the churchyard are memorials to Rowland Denis, ob. 1685, and Richard Dennis, ob. 1783. The register of baptisms dates from the year 1567; marriages and burials, 1548. The living is a vicarage, net yearly value £170, including 52 acres of glebe, with residence, in the gift of and held since 1899 by the Rev. Louis Coutier Biggs M.A. of St. Edmund

The Bell Inn.

Hall, Oxford. There is a Wesleyan and Bible Christian chapel. Annery House, the seat of Mrs. Somes, stands in a finely undulating park, richly timbered, and forms a striking object from the road leading from Bideford to Torrington ; it was formerly the residence of Chief Justice Hankford, whose death (Dec. 20, 1422) is said to have been caused by his own gamekeeper, whom he had disturbed on a dark night, after issuing strict injunctions to him to shoot anyone who should not reply when accosted. Petticombe, the property of Capt. A. J. Saltren-Willett. is at present (1901) unoccupied ; Mrs. Pine-Coffin, of Portledge, who is lady of the manor, Captain A. J. Saltren-Willett, and Mrs. Somes are the chief landowners. The soil is clayey; subsoil, clay. The chief

crops are cereals. The area is 2,163 acres of land, 8 of water, 9 of tidal water, and 2 of foreshore; rateable value, £1,849; the population in 1891 was 429.

Sexton, James Eastman.

Post Office.—Thomas Youatt, sub-postmaster. Letters through Torrington arrive at 8.50 a.m. ; dispatched at 4.30 p.m. week days only. Postal orders are issued here, but not paid. Torrington, 3 miles distant, is the nearest telegraph & money order office

Wall Letter Box, Annery, cleared at 4.15 p.m. week days only

Parochial School (mixed), built in 1875, for 100 children ; average attendance, 51 ; Miss A. H. Anstey, mist

The village children.

Biggs Rev. Louis Coutier M.A. Verge
Cooper Miss Down
Holland John, The Chantry
Somes Mrs. Annery house

COMMERCIAL.

Bond John, farmer, The Barton
Boundy Asa, farmer & water miller
Clarke Silas, gardener to Mrs. Somes
Chapple William, butcher, farmer & cattle dealer, Ley

Cooper John Groves, farmer
Ellis Eliza (Mrs.), shopkeeper
Grigg John, jun. farmer, Lewisham
Grigg John, farmer, Venton
Hearn John, miller (water) & farmer
Hill Thomas, farmer, Town farm
Huxtable James, farmer, Knowle
Newcombe Thos.frmr. West Annery
Partridge Edwd. farmer & auctioneer, land agent & surveyor, agricultural

& general valuer, Annery Barton; & at Bideford
Phillips John, farmer, Orchard
Tucker Edwin, blacksmith
Westaway Richard, farmer, Lodge
Westcott William, Bell inn
Withecombe George, butcher, Annery
Youatt John, wheelwright & smith & assistant overseer

The post office, Monkleigh.

NEWTON ST. PETROCK is a parish and village on the river Torridge, here crossed by a bridge of three arches, to Milton Damerel, 6 miles from Bude canal, 7 south-west from Torrington terminal station of a branch from Barnstaple of the London and South Western railway and 11 south from Bideford, in the North Western division of the county, Shebbear hundred, Bideford petty sessional division, union and county court district, rural deanery of Torrington, archdeaconry of Barnstaple and diocese of Exeter. The church of St. Patrick is a building of stone in the Gothic style, consisting of chancel, nave, south aisle, south porch and an embattled western tower, with pinnacles, 51 feet in height, and containing 3 bells, of which the first is dated 1671; the second and third are respectively inscribed, in Old English characters:— 'Est michi coliatum ℟.℟.℟. istud nomen amatum"; "Me melior vere non est campana sub ere"; the latter, which is the tenor bell, weighs 9 cwt. 2 qrs.: the church contains some very ancient carved oak benches, bearing the shields of Prideaux, Hatch, Grenville and others; the church was restored and enlarged in 1887, under the direction of Mr. Samuel Hooper, architect, of Hatherleigh, at a total cost of £618, when the chancel was extended eastwards 3 feet: the former pews were removed and the church reseated with benches, in which the ancient woodwork as well as a quantity of carved oak discovered beneath the flooring was incorporated; some of this was used in the construction of a new pulpit, the panels of which display the emblems of the Passion; the rood loft stairs and the doorway leading thereto now form the entrance to the pulpit: the roofs and most of the windows are now: new pinnacles have been placed on the tower and its western arch opened to the nave: there are 150 sittings. The register of baptisms and marriages dates from the year 1578; burials, 1737. The living is a rectory, net yearly value £175, including 77 acres of glebe with residence, in the gift of and held since 1895 by the Rev. Francis Walter Hobbs B.A. of Worcester College, Oxford. There is a Baptist chapel, built in 1862. The Rev. F. W. Hobbs M.A. who is lord of the manor, John Curzon Moore-Stevens esq. of Winscott, and Mrs. C. Tucker, of Holsworthy, are the chief landowners. The soil is clayey; the subsoil, clay. The chief crops are wheat, barley and oats. The area is 1,981 acres; rateable value, £1,034; the population in 1891 was 234 in the civil and 219 in the ecclesiastical parish.

By Local Government Board Order 14,831, a detached part of Frithelstock parish, in Torrington union, known as Great and Little Cleave and Dovies, was transferred to this parish, March 25, 1885, for civil purposes.

Letters received by foot post from Torrington at 12 noon & from Brandis Corner R.S.O. at 9.30 a.m. The nearest money order & telegraph office is at Shebbear, 3 miles distant

Letter Box cleared at 12.50 p.m. daily, sundays excepted

This place is included in the United School Board district of Shebbear and Newton St. Petrock, formed Sept. 8, 1874, consisting of 5 members; W. W. Daniel, Backway, Shebbear, clerk to the board

Board School (mixed), built, with residence for the master, in 1875, at a cost of £700, for 65 children; average attendance, 42; Walter Cann, master

(Marked thus * letters should be addressed Brandis Corner R.S.O.)
*Hobbs Rev. Fras. Walt. B.A. Rectry

COMMERCIAL.
Blight Alfred, blacksmith
Blight Wm. (Mrs.), farmr. Down fm
Brooks William, carpenter
Buse Isaac, cowkeeper, Bullator
Cleveland Richard, farmer, Venn
Ellis Augustus Albert, butcher
Ellis Edward James, wheelwright
*Fishleigh James, farmer, West hole
Fowler George, farmer, Slew
Fowler William, farmer, Hockwill
Harris Edgar, farmer, Cleave
Hearn John, farmer, Holwell
Hole John, farmer, East hole
Hooper Isaac, farmer
Leverton James, cowkpr. Sanctuary
Manning John, farmer, Bullator
Quance John, farmer, Sutton
*Quance William, farmer, Lane Barton
*Slade Geo.frmr.West hole & Coombe
*Slade James, farmer, Bridge farm
Slade James, jun, farmer, Ford
Slade William, miller (water)
Squire John, farmer, Down moor

The cottage by the church.

The Village. Newton Tracey

Looking up through the village, the old post office is on the right.

NEWTON TRACEY is a parish and village, on the old road leading from Torrington to Barnstaple, and adjoining Fremington, 3½ miles from Instow station on the Torrington branch of the North Devon section of the London and South Western railway and 4½ south-west from Barnstaple, in the North Western division of the county, Fremington hundred, Braunton petty sessional division, Barnstaple union and county court district, and in the rural deanery and archdeaconry of Barnstaple and diocese of Exeter. The church of St. Thomas à Becket is a small but ancient building in the Perpendicular style, consisting of chancel, nave, north aisle, south porch and an embattled western tower containing 3 bells; the two first bear legends in Old English characters; the tenor, a beautiful recasting, has the name "Gabriel" and an invocation to the Virgin in Lombardic type: the church was restored in 1868 and a north aisle added, when some curious and ancient wall paintings were found in the chancel, but owing to the insecure condition of the walls, they were destroyed; there are 94 sittings. The register of baptisms dates from the year 1566; marriages, 1570;

burials, 1562. The living is a rectory, net yearly value £77, with 36 acres of glebe, in the gift of the Lord Chancellor, and held since 1870 by the Rev. John Dene B.A. of St. John's College, Oxford, who is also rector of and resides at Horwood. Newton House is the property and seat of James Paton esq. lord of the manor; J. Paton esq. and the Rev. Thomas Poltimore Dimond Hogg M.A. vicar of Saltney, Chester, are the principal landowners. The soil is good loam; the subsoil is clay. The chief crops are wheat, barley and oats. The area is 338 acres; assessable value, £418; the population in 1901 was 126.

Parish Clerk, William Pickard.

Post Office.—William Symons, sub-postmaster. Letters received from Barnstaple at 8.35 a.m.; dispatched at 4.50 p.m. No arrival or dispatch on sundays. Postal orders are issued here, but not paid. The nearest money order & telegraph office is at Barnstaple, 5 miles distant

This place is included in the Horwood United School Board district, formed February 4, 1875.

The children of this parish attend the Board school at Loveacott

Edger Mrs
Paton James J.P. Newton house
COMMERCIAL.
Balman William, butcher
Chamings Nicholas, cattle dealer

Ford Alfred, farmer, Glebe
Ford John, farmer, Barton
Hedge John, farmer, Cobblestone
Holmes George, Hunter's inn
Mugridge George, mason

Pickard William, wheelwright
Symons William, jun. blacksmith
Symons Wm. shopkeeper, Post office
Yeo William, cattle dealer

General View. Newton Tracey

A general view of the village.

Lovacott children on a Sunday school outing, c. 1910.

The school house, Lovacott.

The village and the Hunter's Inn, Newton Tracey.

NORTH LEW is a compact village and parish, 2¼ miles north from Ashbury and North Lew station on the Okehampton and Holsworthy branch of the London and South Western railway, 4¾ south-west from Hatherleigh and 7 north-west from Okehampton, in the Western division of the county, petty sessional division of Hatherleigh, hundred of Black Torrington, union of Okehampton, county court district of Totnes, rural deanery of Okehampton, archdeaconry of Totnes and diocese of Exeter. The river Lew, which flows through the parish, abounds in salmon and trout. The church of St. Thomas à Becket is a building of stone, chiefly in the Perpendicular style, with some earlier portions, and consists of chancel, nave, aisles, south porch and an embattled western tower, with pinnacles, containing 5 bells: the great feature of the interior is the very fine carving of the benches, dating from the 16th century and exhibiting great diversity of design and elaborate workmanship: the ends of the benches bear in some cases the emblems of the Passion and in others shields with monograms and the date 1537.: the roofs are also of carved oak and the lower portion of the rood screen remains: the stained east window was presented by the late Miss Woollcombe, of Morth Grange, and there are oak choir stalls and lectern, introduced at the late restoration: the font, an interesting example of Norman work, is assumed to have belonged to the original church: in 1894 a carved stone reredos was erected as a memorial to the late Miss Woollcombe, of Morth Grange a new organ has since been provided by public subscription: the church was restored in 1885 at a cost of £1,450, under the direction of Mr. R. Medley Fulford A.R.I.B.A. of Exeter. when the roofs and benches were carefully repaired by Mr. H. Hems, of Exeter, the flooring relaid, a new communion table, pulpit, lectern and choir stalls erected, the battle-menting of the tower renewed and the fabric generally renovated: a number of ancient embossed tiles have been laid down in the tower: the church affords 239 sittings. The register dates from the year 1700. The living is a rectory united with Ashbury, joint net yearly value £450. with 74 acres of glebe here and residence, in the gift of the Crown, and held since 1885 by the Rev. John Worthington M.A. of Brasenose College, Oxford, and rural dean of Okehampton. There are Bible Christian and Wesleyan chapels, also a Bible Christian Sunday school, erected in 1890. In the village is an ancient stone cross, to which a new granite shaft was added in 1900 by H. Hems and Sons, of Exeter. William Madge esq. of Blagdon, and the rector are lords of the manor. Morth Grange belongs to Mrs. George Woollcombe. John Morth Woollcombe esq. of Ashbury House, Mrs. George Woollcombe, and the trustees of the late Ven. Archdeacon Henry Woollcombe are landowners here. The soil is sand and clay; subsoil, stone. The chief crops are wheat, barley, oats and roots. The area is 7,247 acres of land and 12 of water; rateable value, £3,830; the population in 1901 was 629.

Sexton, Alexander Horn.

Post, M. O. & T. O., T. M. O.. Express Delivery, Parcel Post, S. B. & Annuity & Insurance Office.—Mrs. Fanny Gay, sub-postmistress. Letters received from Beaworthy R.S.O. North Devon, at 7.50 a.m.; dispatched at 5 p.m

Devon Constabulary, Henry William Bebbings, constable

National School (mixed), built in 1866, for 160 children; average attendance, 98; Henry Venton, master; Mrs. Venton, infant mistress; Miss Wood, mistress

The bridge, Northlew.

A maypole dance in the Rectory garden, c. 1911. Note the smocks. The girl on the far left is Dorothy Spier, beside her is John Adams.

The Armistice Ragtime Band, 1918. From left to right: Bert Pascoe, ? Badcock, Gilbert Scant, Archie King, Morris Scant, Tom Andrew, Louis Adams, Bill Hortop, Edgar Dufty. In the front are Charlie Curtis and Bill Watkins.

Adams William
Budge James, Dingley house
Dennis Mrs. West Worth
Cocks Rev. Walter (Bible Christian)
Cox Mrs. Elmfield
Hardy Miss
Medley Mrs. Winsford Towers
Shellabear John
Woollcombe Mrs. Geo. Morth grange
Worthington Rev. John M.A. (rector & rural dean), Rectory

COMMERCIAL.

Adams Henry, farmer, Kesterfield
Andrews Thos. whlwrght. & carpentr
Baker John & Sons, blacksmiths
Baker James, farmer, Lands end
Bater John, carpenter & wheelwright, Southyeo cottage
Bater John, farmer, Southyeo
Bater Robert, farmer, East Southyeo
Bater Thomas farmer, Whiddon
Bickle William, farmer, West Kimbr
Blatchford John, mason
Breyley James, yeoman
Breyley Emma (Miss), shopkeeper
Brooking John, shopkeeper

Brooking Nicholas, cattle dealer
Brooking Thomas, farmer
Brooking William, farmer, Crowden
Crocker Henry, farmer, New moor
Crocker Jas. cowkeeper, Graddon
Cudmore Samuel, Green Dragon P.H
Curtis Thomas, cowkeeper
Dennis Charlotte (Miss), farmer, West Worth
Dufty Benj. farmer, West Southyeo
Dymond Wm. farmr. Ruthleigh Bartn
Evely Henry, miller (water) & farmer, & registrar of births & deaths for Bratton Clovelly district, Okehampton union, Crowden
Evely John, deputy registrar of births & deaths for Bratton Clovelly district, Okehampton union, Crowden
Friend John & Son, farmers, Crowden
Friend Arthur, farmer, West Worth
Friend Henry Jn. farmer, Churchgte
Friend James, farmer, Loveland
Friend Walter Wm. road contractor
Gay William, farmer, Lake
Glass Wm. & Son, farmers & millers (water), Lew mill

Glass Edward, millwright
Gloyn Edward Rich, yeoman, Norley
Gloyn William Henry, farmer, Norley
Harry John, farmer, Milltown
Harry Joseph, farmer, Higher Whitton
Harry Thos. farmer, Lower East Worth
Heggadon Evan, farmer, Bolland
Heggadon John, farmer, East Kimber
Hill James, farmer, Stone quarry
Lashbrook William, carpenter, Fordatown hills
Lovell John, farmer, Lower Gorhuish
Martin John, shoe maker & farmer
Martin William John, butcher & farmer, Southcombe
May John, farmer, Palmer's Norley
Moyse William, farmer, Furze hill
Northcott Thomas, farmer, Higher Eastcott
Passmore George F. farmer, Lambert farms
Pellew Henry, assistant overseer & school attendance officer
Phare Henry, farmer, Birch lane
Post Henry John, farmer, Worth
Sanders Edwin & William, tailors

The old cross and church. The children probably belonged to the Friend family. This photograph was taken before the cross was altered.

Shobbrook William, farmer & mason
Skinner John, farmer, Lower Eastcott
Smale John, farmer, Southcombe
Smale Thos. & Rd. farmers, Durdon
Smale Albert, farmer, Eastacombe
Smale Fdk.Geo.yeoman, Sth.Whiddon
Smale James, farmer, Crowden

Smale John, Honychurch Arms P.H
Smale Wm.farmr.Howards Gorhuish
Smallacombe Geo. farmer, We. Kimber
Tom Thomas, farmer, Blackworthy
Vallance Thomas, farmer, Heath
Voaden William, farmer, Kimber
Voaden William, farmer, Arrathorne

West John, farmer, Slate quarry
White William, farmer, Green down
Wood Samuel & Son, tailors
Wood Thomas, grocer & draper
WooldridgeHy.carpntr. & wheelwright
Wooldridge Thomas, farmer, Whiddon

John, Mary Ann and Thomas Baker at North Lew forge, c. 1900.

The school.

NORTH MOLTON is a parish and long straggling village, seated on the side of a hill on the borders of Exmoor and on the river Mole, from which it derives its name, 2½ miles north-east from South Molton station on the Devon and Somerset branch of the Great Western railway and 12 east from Barnstaple, in the Northern division of the county, South Molton hundred, petty sessional division, union and county court district, rural deanery of South Molton, archdeaconry of Barnstaple and diocese of Exeter. This parish is the second largest in Devon. The church of All Saints, standing on an eminence, is a building of stone in the Perpendicular style, consisting of chancel with chapels, clerestoried nave of four bays, aisles, south porch and an embattled western tower 100 feet high, with pinnacles, and containing a clock and 6 bells : there is a carved oak screen and a fine font of Perpendicular date with an octagonal basin, richly arcaded, on a shaft adorned with canopied niches containing effigies : the pulpit is of oak, elaborately carved with figures of saints : on the south side of the tower, under a canopy, is a large figure of the Virgin and Child : the east window is stained : in the south aisle is a memorial window to William Davy : and in 1894 another was placed to the late Rev. William Burdett, formerly vicar here :

In the parish are several mines, at one time worked for copper, iron, silver, lead and gold, traces of which were met with about 1840. This parish has long been celebrated for its breed of North Devon cattle. A cattle fair is held on the first Wednesday after May 12th and the last Wednesday in October. There are almshouses for six poor people, founded by Mr. Parker, and various bequests for the benefit of the poor, amounting to £20 yearly.

FLITTON, 2½ miles north-west ; FYLDON, 3½ north ; HEASLEY, 2 north ; UPCOTT, 1 east ; WALSCOTT, 2 north-west ; HUNSTON, 3½ miles north-west, and BENT-WITCHEN, 4 miles north, are hamlets of this parish.

Sexton, Thomas Loosemore.

Police Station, James Ireland, constable

Post, M. O. & T. O., T. M. O., Express Delivery, Parcel Post, S. B. & Annuity & Insurance Office.—George Henry Holloway, sub-postmaster. Letters are received through South Molton at 7.35 a.m. ; dispatched 6 p.m. ; sundays, arrive 7.35 a.m. ; dispatched 10.15 a.m. The letter box is also cleared in the morning for the district

Wall Letter Boxes at Fyldon cleared at 4.45 ; Heasley mill, 5.10 ; Mole bridge, 5.30

A School Board of 5 members was formed May 26, 1874 ; Frederick Dobbs, clerk to the board & attendance officer

The Square.

North Molton Church.

Davey Henry, butcher, The Square
Davey James, farmer, Briton farm
Dobbs F. & Son, auctioneers & valuers, seedsmen, general agricultural mers. & millers (water roller)
Fishleigh Samuel Andrew, farmer, Brown's Marsh
Frayne Peter, draper & grocer
Gammon John Bright, farmer, Little Combeshead
Gammon Thos. Jn. farmr. Low.Poole
Garner Charles, farmer, Lower Ley
German Fredk. farmer, Marsh house
Gold James, farmer, Oakford
Gould George Alfd. farmer, Walscott
Govier John W. boot maker
Govier George, thatcher
Handford George, gamekeeper to Lord Poltimore P.C. Barham
Hanford Sarah (Mrs.), dress maker
Harding Elizabeth (Mrs.) & William, farmers, Millbrook
Haydon Francis Wm.farmer, Yardgate
Haydon Wm. farmer,Great Combshead
Hayes James & William, farmers, Berkham
Hayes Mary Mrs.), farmer, West Brinsworthy
Hill James, farmer, Tabor hill
Holloway George Henry, blacksmith, Post office
Hutchings Geo.blacksmith, Heasley ml
Hutchings Jn.farmer, Longstone wells
Huxtable Francis, boot & shoe maker, Heasley mill
Jackson William Roy M.A. St. And., M.B. & C.M.Edin. physician & surgeon, medical officer & public vac-

cinator Nos. 2 & 5 districts, South Molton union
Kingdon Wm. farmr. ThornesHeasley
Knight Geo. farmer, Higher Hunston
Lock Wm. Jas. grocer & draper
Locke James, Poltimore Arms P.H
Loosemore William, boot maker
Martin Elizabeth (Mrs.), miller (water) & shopkpr. Heasley mill
Merson Jn.Nott,farmr.Ea. Brinsworthy
Newton James, farmer, Rapscott
Newton William, farmer, Holdridge
Newton William, farmer, Rapscott
North Molton Social Club (Lord Poltimore, president; Rev. Canon Woodman & F. W. Wreford, vice-presidents; Fredk. Dobbs, hon. sec)
Parkin Francis, farmer, Upcott
Passmore Charles Avery, saddler
Passmore John, carrier
Passmore William, farmer, Buttery
Purchase Daniel Nicholas, farmer, South Radworthy
Rew Thomas, yeoman, commissioner of land & income taxes, Sannacott
Richards George, farmer, Flitton
Robins William, farmer, Great Heasley
Rudd George & William, farmers, Shortacombe
Rudd John, farmer, North Radworthy
Sanders Frederick ,farmer,Hunnawins
Sanders Richd. farmer, Low. Hunstn
Scott Ann (Mrs.), dress maker
Scott John, farmer, Bullens
Slader John, farmer, Higher Ley
Smith Eliza (Miss), dress maker, Lower Lodge

Slader John, farmer, East Marsh
Smith Joseph Denner, carpenter
Smyth Charles, boot maker
Smyth William, farmer & landowner, Ben Twitchen
Somerville Alvan,coal dlr.frmr.&btchr
Stanbury George, farmer, Litchaton
Stoneman Richd. Bird,frmr.Bornacott
Stranger Richard John, estate agent to LordPoltimore & farmr.Court ho
Thorne James & Geo. farmers, East yd
Thorne George,jun.farmer,Witheygate
Thorne John, farmer, West yard
Thorne John R. farmer, Lower Fyldon
Thorne Thomas, farmer, Beera
Thorne Thos. farmer, Higher Fyldon
Thorne Thos.H.farmr. Crosscomb dwn
Treble Mary (Mrs.), dress maker
Watts John, Poltimore Arms P.H. Yard down
Webber Mark, farmer, North Heasley
Westcott Catherine (Miss), dress maker, The Square
Westcott Charles, farmer, Old house
Westcott Elizabeth (Mrs.), china & earthenware dealer
Westcott Henry, farmer, Wheatland
Westcott Nicholas, frmr. Sth. Barton
Westcott Robert Holcombe, farmer, West park
Westcott Robt.jun. farmer, North Lee
Westcott William, farmer, Back lane
Wreford Frederick William,estate clerk of works to Lord Poltimore
Yendell Frederick S. farmer, Nadrid
Yendell John L. farmer, Upcott
Yendell Joseph, farmer, South Heasley

NORTH TAWTON is a small market town and parish near the old road from Exeter to Okehampton, and on the river Taw, which is here crossed by a bridge of four arches, leading to Hatherleigh and Okehampton, with a station on the London and South Western railway, 1¼ miles south from the town, and is 20 miles north-west from Exeter, 12 west from Crediton, 8 east-by-south from Hathersleigh, 7 north-east from Okehampton and 190¾ from London, in the Northern division of the county, North Tawton hundred, South Molton petty sessional division, Okehampton union and county court district, rural deanery of Okehampton, archdeaconry of Totnes and diocese of Exeter. Water was conveyed into the town from Slade farm, through iron pipes, in the year 1851, at an expense of £600, raised in shares of £5 each, and the Okehampton Rural District Council have since taken steps to provide a further supply, at a cost of £2,500; gas works were erected in 1869, at a cost of £750, and are the property of Henry Gibbings esq. A complete system of drainage was carried out in 1894-5, under the superintendence of Edward Ellis C.E. of Exeter, at a cost of £700. The church of St. Peter is an ancient building of rubble and granite, in the Perpendicular style,

There is a Congregational chapel, erected in 1834, with 300 sittings; one for Bible Christians, seating 150 persons; and a meeting-room for Plymouth Brethren, with 60 sittings. The Market-house was erected in 1849; petty sessions are held here alternately with Chulmleigh. A clock tower of red brick with freestone dressings, from designs by Mr. R. Medley Fulford, architect, of Exeter, was erected in the square by public subscription in 1887, at a cost of £130. Here are large woollen mills, a branch factory belonging to Messrs. J. Shaw and Sons Limited, of Halifax, enlarged in 1887, and employing about 150 persons in the manufacture of serges and top making; here also are Mr. J. C. Tavener's flour mills, which are lit by electricity. The market is held on Thursday. Fairs for cattle and horses are held on the 3rd Tuesday in April, 2nd Tuesday in October and a fat stock show 1st Tuesday in December, and great markets are held on the last Thursdays in February and June, and 1st Thursday in August. On the hill overlooking the town is a wooden house brought from Norway, the property and residence of Lady Constable. About a mile from the town is a hollow in the ground called "Bathe Pool," usually dry, but which occasionally fills with water and overflows.

A view of the Square. The clock tower was erected in 1887.

A general view of the town.

County Police Station, Sergeant Thomas Gammon, in charge & 1 constable

Sexton, William Oliver Priest

PUBLIC OFFICERS.

Assistant Overseer & Collector of Taxes, John Ellis Pyke

Clerk to Commissioners of Taxes, George L. Fulford

Certifying Factory Surgeon, Medical Officer & Public Vaccinator, North Tawton District, Okehampton Union, Montagu Cutcliffe M.R.C.S.Eng., L.R.C.P.Lond

Registrar of Births & Deaths for North Tawton Sub-district, Okehampton Union, John Ellis Pyke; deputy registrar, Edward Goss

Inland Revenue Officer, Alfred W. Norton

Town Crier, John Skinner, Exeter street

SCHOOLS.

A School Board of 5 members was formed Feb. 21, 1872; Edward Goss, clerk to the board; attendance officer, George Davey, North Tawton

Board (boys & girls), built in 1875, for 300 children; average attendance, 80 boys & 75 girls; James Chanter Pierce, master; Sarah Louisa Pierce, mistress

Board (infants), acquired in 1875, & holding 125 children; average attendance, 76; Miss Kate Bowden, mistress

Railway Station, George Risbridger, station master

Agents to South Western Railway Co. Lewis & Son

Omnibus from 'Ring of Bells' meets all trains

Carriers.—Weekes, through from Hatherleigh to Exeter, thurs. returning sat.; Ball, daily from Hatherleigh to North Tawton station

A group of children lined up across the Square before the clock tower was built. The stone pillar on the right is now in the churchyard, c. 1875.

The Square, North Tawton. A similar view to the picture above, probably taken about 30 years later.

North Street. The coalman with his cart is Mr Northcott. Mr Fisher, the carpenter, is standing on the left. It is interesting to note that both these names occur in the list opposite.

Barton Lane; the Co-op stores, which was kept by Miss Bennett.

Seaward Miss. Fore street
Snell William J.P. Broad Nymet (letters should be addressed Bow R.S.O)
Tavener Jas. Camble J.P. Melhuishes
Taylor Rev. Thomas Henry (Congregational), Tennis court
Thompson Thomas, Burton hall
Tucker Samuel James, Exeter street

COMMERCIAL.

Anstey Harry, White Hart inn
Attwell Frank, baker
Attwell Charles, Fountain inn
Avery John, shopkeeper
Axford Thomas James, farmer, Nichols Nymet
Banberry Bessie (Miss), shopkeeper, Fore street
Banbery Thomas, builder, High street
Bastow Louisa (Miss), dress maker, Fore street
Bickham William Davis, farmer & jobmaster, Park terrace
Bolt Richard, shopkeeper, North st
Bonner Edward, grocer & provision dealer, The Square
Bowden Wm. shoe maker, High street
Bowden Thomas, shoe maker, High st
Bradford Thomas, baker, Fore street
Brown Richard, farmer, Week
Chambers Walter Ernest, Railway inn
Choat George, blacksmith, Fore st
Curry Henry, Gostwyck Arms P.H
Cutcliffe Montagu M.R.C.S.Eng., L.R.C.P.Lond. surgeon & medical officer & public vaccinator North Tawton district, Okehampton union & certifying factory surgeon, Court green
Darch Jesse & Son, saddlers, Fore st
Dart Eliza (Mrs.),& Son,frmrs Bridge
Dart Thos. Luxton,jun.frmr.High st
Daw Thomas, farmer, Greenslade (letters should be addressed Sampford Courtenay R.S.O)
Day Lewis William, aërated water manufacturer, Essington
Day Wm. Geo. blacksmith, High st
Densem Thomas George Ellis, commercial traveller, Moor view
Devon & Cornwall Banking Co. Lim. (sub-branch of) (open on thursdays & fair days); draw on Barclay & Co. Lim. London E C
Dingley, Pearse & Co. (Okehampton Bank) (sub-branch); open thursdays & fair days only; draw on London City & Midland Bank Limited, London E C
Down Frank, farmer, Beere
Drew Mary Jane & Susanna (Misses), stationers & fancy repository
Dulling Henry Jas. tailor, The Square
Durant, Avery & Merchant, threshing machine proprs.; & at Bow R.S.O
Durant & Sons, seed growers
Ellis Samuel & Sons, builders & contractors, Fore street
Evans Samuel, butcher, Fore street
Fisher Bros. builders & contractors, North street

Folland Thomas, farmer, Wardens
Ford Wm. road contractor, North st
Fulford George Langdon, solicitor, commissioner for oaths, clerk to the commissioners of taxes & to the school board at Sampford Courtenay & acting clerk to magistrates, North Tawton district; & at Okehampton Gas Works (Henry Gibbings, propr)
Gibbings John Henson, farmer, Week
Gibbings John Durant & Son, btchrs. Market street
Gibbings Robert, farmer, Upcott (letters should be addressed Bow R.S.O)
Gorwyn Albt. Lambert, frmr. Halse
Goss Edward, accountant, deputy registrar of births & deaths for North Tawton sub-district & clerk to the school board & agent for Liverpool & London & Globe, Fire & Economic Life & for the Ocean Accident Co
Goss Florence & Emily (Misses), girls' day school, The Square
Hannaford Roger, confr. High street
Hannaford Samuel, farmer, Slade
Heard Wm. hair dresser, Exeter st
Heath Jane (Mrs.), shopkpr. High st
Heath William John, Ring of Bells, every accommodation for commercials & visitors; posting in all its branches; 'bus meets all trains
Hirst William, branch manager to John Shaw & Son Lim.woollen mfrs
Hoyle Samuel, branch manager to John Shaw & Son Limited, woollen manufacturers
James William, farmer, Bathe
Knight William ,butcher, The Square
Lee John, shoe maker, Barton street
Letheren Charley, grocer & draper
Lewis & Son, carriers & agents for the London & South Western Railway Co. High street
Long William, dairyman, Fore street
Lovell William, blacksmith, Paffords
Madge Philip & Sons,butchers,High st
Manning Thomas George & Son, irongers
Martin Wm. chimney swpr. High st
May Ernest, farmer, Crooke
May George Hall, farmer, Westacott
Metherell Joseph, relieving & vaccination officer for North Tawton district, Okehampton union
Mitchell John, dairyman, Southwick
National Provincial Bank of England Limited (sub-branch of); open on thursdays & fair days: draw on head office, 112 Bishopsgate within, London E C
Northcott Fredk. coal dealer,Exeter st
North Tawton Co-operative Society Limited (Tom O. Bennett, sec)
Norton Alfd. W.inland revenue officer
Paddon Thomas, wool dealer & farmer, Farwells
Phillips & Son, devon serge wareho
Pilman Jonas, lessee of fair tolls, North street

Pizzey George Vilven, tailor, High st
Potter & Sons, machinists, Exeter st
Powlesland George, farmer, Lower Nichols Nymet
Pyke, Powlesland & Son, auctioneers
Pyke J. & M. drapers, Fore street
Pyke John, auctioneer, see Pyke, Powlesland & Son
Pyke John Ellis, accountant & registrar of births & deaths for North Tawton sub-district, assistant overseer, collector of taxes & agent for Norwich Union Insurance Society
Rattenbury Hugh, shopkpr. High st
Reading & Recreation Rooms (Charley Letheren, sec)
Sampson Charles, builder, High street
Saunders Saml. Jn. butcher,Exeter st
Searle Samuel, farmer, Lower stone
Shaw John & Sons Limited, woollen manufacturers (William Hirst & Samuel Hoyle, branch managers); head office, Halifax, Yorks
Short Wm. farmer & aparts. Barton
Skinner Frank, grocer & post office & agent for Sun Fire & Life Insurance Society
Skinner John, town crier & bill poster, Exeter street
Skinner William, chemist
Sloman William, farmer, Staddon
Snell William, farmer, Broad Nymet (letters should be addressed Bow R.S.O)
Squire Martha (Mrs.), boot dealer & news agent, Fore street
Stone Bros. farmers, Ashridge
Stoneman William, farmer & dairyman, Essington
Tamlin Susanna (Mrs.), draper & grocer, The Square
Tamlin Thomas, ironmonger, The Sq
Tamlin Lucy & Ophelia (Misses), fancy drapers, The Square
Tavener James Camble, miller (water & steam), Newland mills
Taylor James, thatcher, Barton street
Taylor John, chimney swpr. Fore st
Taylor Saml. farmer, Tawton wood
Taylor Samuel, shoe maker, High st
Taylor Thomas, coal dealer, Exeter st
Taylor William, mason
Tucker John, dairyman & farmer, Middle stone
Turner John, thatcher, East street
Vanstone Richard, dairyman, Moors
Vilven Joshua, tailor
Vooght Susan Ann (Mrs.), farmer, Sandford
Ward & Co.coal & general merchants, Railway station (branch)
Way Francis, shopkeeper, High street
Webber George, farmer, Yeo
West Tom Percival, teacher of music & organist of the parish church, Park terrace
Willcocks Charles, Globe inn
Willcocks Eliza (Miss), baker,High st
Willcocks John, wheelwright & carpenter, High street

Exeter Street. I think this is the earlier of the two photographs.

Exeter Street.

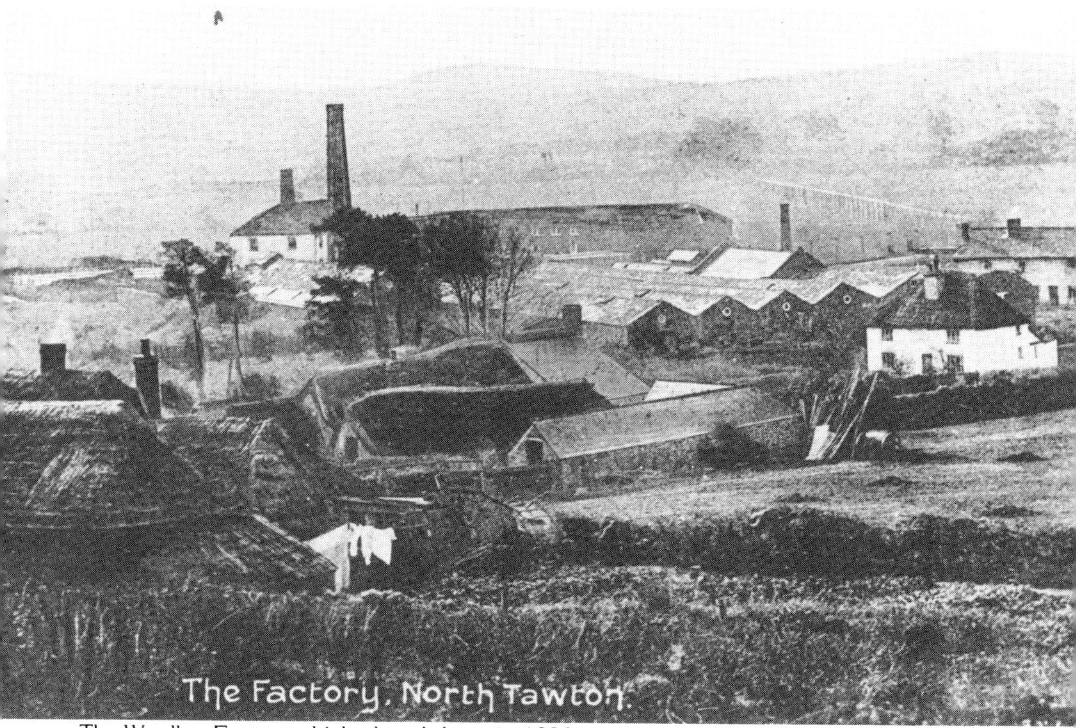

The Factory, North Tawton.

The Woollen Factory which closed down in 1930.

Exeter Street, North Tawton

Exeter Street.

High Street.

Coronation Day, 1911, in Exeter Street. The lady in the foreground on the far left is Mrs Sanders of No. 12 Fore Street, North Tawton. The lady next to her on the right is her mother, Mrs Salter, and the man with the beard is a Mr Ellis.

The old Smithy, now no longer in existence.

The Devon Serge warehouse.

A group of children outside a fire-gutted house in 1908.

A foxhound meet outside the old Goswyke House in the Square, 1911.

LSWR station, c. 1914.

A group of Rechabites, c. 1895. The Rechabites (originally a tribe of Israel) are a free church movement promoting total abstinence.

OKEHAMPTON (or Oakhampton) is an ancient municipal borough, market and union town and the head of a county court district, on the East and West Okement rivers, on the high road from Exeter into Cornwall, adjoining Dartmoor, with a station on the main line of the London and South Western railway, and is 22 miles west-by-north from Exeter, 30 north-by-east from Plymouth, 16 north-north-east from Tavistock, 19½ north-east from Launceston, 22 east-by-south from Holsworthy and 197½ by rail, via Exeter, from London, in the Western division of the county, partly in the Lifton and partly in the Black Torrington hundred, Hatherleigh petty sessional division, rural deanery of Okehampton, archdeaconry of Totnes and diocese of Exeter. The town, incorporated by charters granted by James I. in 1623 and Charles II. in 1684, was formerly governed by a mayor, recorder, eight principal and eight assistant burgesses; but under the provisions of Schedule I. of the Municipal Corporation Act, 1882 (45 and 46 Vict. c. 50) the then Corporation became extinct, and the inhabitants petitioned for a new charter, which was granted 24 June, 1885, and the Corporation now consists of a mayor, four aldermen and twelve councillors. Under Section 1, sub-section 3, of the "Local Government Act, 1894" (56 and 57 Vict. c. 73), the parish was divided, namely:—Okehampton Borough and Okehampton Hamlets, or rural.

The town is well lighted with gas by a company formed in 1858 with a capital of £1,200. The electric light was also adopted in 1885, and additional plant laid down in 1889 and in 1896. The inhabitants are supplied with water by high pressure from a reservoir dependent on springs on the Okehampton Park estate, adjoining the town on the south, and in 1893 the Local Government Board granted the sum of £800 for the purpose of increasing the supply. A complete system of drainage was carried out in 1886-7 by the new Corporation, under the superintendence of Edward Appleton C.E. of Torquay, at a cost of £2,300. In 1887 the east bridge was widened 10 feet and about two-thirds of the town repaved, at a cost of £1,850: the Local Government Board also sanctioned a further loan of £400 for paving the footpath between the town and the railway station, but the town is now paved throughout. The church of All Saints, originally built in 1261, was rebuilt in the 15th century and again in 1844, under the direction of Mr. Hayward, architect, of Exeter, the old church, with the exception of the tower, having been destroyed by fire in 1842: it is now an edifice of stone in the Perpendicular style, consisting of chancel with vestry on the north side, nave of five bays, aisles, north and south porches and an embattled western tower, with crocketed pinnacles, containing 6 bells, cast in the churchyard in 1750: there is a good octagonal panelled font: the tower is Transitional and Late Decorated:

Fore Street, Okehampton.

The March Fair, 1907.

The Market, at the back of the Town Hall, forms an extensive range of spacious buildings, with ample conveniences. A butter and poultry hall was erected in 1880, at a cost of £1,000; and further improvements, including a room for technical instruction, were carried out in 1893 at a cost of £400, of which amount £200 was contributed by the County Council. The principal support of the town arises from its market, large quantities of agricultural produce being forwarded to all parts. Saturday is the market day, and a great cattle market is held on the first Saturday in every month. The market tolls are let for £358. A fair for cattle is held within the borough on the second Tuesday after March 11th, and a horse fair in October. The Workmen's Club, in St. James' street, contains reading and recreation rooms; there are about 60 members. A swimming bath, 100 feet by 30 feet, was erected by a company in 1890 in the Western Park, opposite the castle; the water, obtained from the hillside, is kept fresh by the maintenance of a constant flow through the bath. In 1895 a drinking fountain of granite was erected in Station road, as a memorial to William Trevor-Roper and Marion Luxmoore, by Mrs. E. C. Trevor-Roper, his widow, and sister of M. Luxmoore. Only two flour mills and one small bone manure factory are at work here. The cabinet making works of Mr. Geen employ a number of hands. An Agricultural Association was formed here in 1890 and 1891, meetings being held at the Town Hall. The White Hart hotel, on the Parade, has spacious coffee and dining rooms and private sitting and billiard rooms, together with very extensive stabling. There are also substantial and comfortable inns, including "The Red Lion," the "Plume of Feathers," "London," and the Temperance hotel.

An early view of the Square.

SCHOOLS.

A School Board of 5 members was formed December 15, 1871, for Okehampton, & re-formed, with an addition of 2 members, Jan. 9, 1872, for Okehampton Borough & Okehampton Hamlets; Charles Sprague, 1 West st. clerk to the board

School, North street (girls & infants), reconstructed in 1874 & enlarged in 1877, at a cost of £1,670, for 400 children; in 1895-6 two class-rooms were added at a cost of about £800; average attendance, 150 girls & 126 infants; Miss Mary Sarah Young, mistress; Mrs. Ada M. Roach, infants' mistress

School, East street (boys), erected in 1896-7 at a cost of about £1,650, for 220 boys; average attendance, 170; George F. Bradley, master

School, Fowley Down (mixed), erected in 1896 at a cost of about £650, for 60 children; average attendance, 35; Miss Lucy Stratford, mistress

CONVEYANCES.

Railway Station, Frank Russell, station master

Colwill's omnibus from Hatherleigh to Okehampton station at 11 a.m. daily, returning at 4 p.m

Garish's omnibus from Chagford to Okehampton station at 11 a.m. mon. wed. & sat. in summer & saturdays only in winter, returning at 4 p.m

Omnibuses from White Hart & London hotels meet all trains

CARRIERS.

Clement, from Chagford, sat. returning same day, George inn

Cooper, from Sticklepath & South Zeal, sat. 'Plume of Feathers'

Mudge, from Drewsteignton, sat. returning same day, Fountain inn

Warren, from Lew Down, sat. returning same day, Plume of Feathers inn

The Royal Artillery arriving in 1894. Kelly states that 'Okehampton Park, consisting of 1050 acres belongs jointly to Mrs Trevor-Roper and Mrs Lees . . . having been purchased in 1780 by Charles Luxmore . . . from the Earl of Devon; ninety acres have been leased for a term of 999 years, for the use of the Royal Horse and Field Artillery, who encamp and practise here for about five months annually; there are permanent stables and other buildings'.

A banquet to celebrate Queen Victoria's Golden Jubilee in 1887.

A morning ramble on 1 May. The townsfolk would get up at 6 a.m. and walk four to five miles – a similar occasion to 'beating the bounds'. Mr Passmore is the white-haired gentleman on the left.

Guy's posting stables, c. 1902.

PRIVATE RESIDENTS.

Abell Thomas, 4 Fair Place terrace
Bate William, Myrtle villa, New road
Bawden Thomas, 7 New road

Clarke Charles Thomson, Parade
Collins Robert, Claremont, Station rd
Cudmore John Badcock, Kempley rd
Davis Miss, 9 Brandis park
Drew Miss, Castle lane
Duffy Bryan, Fair Place terrace
Dunn Edwin, Oakfield, Station road
Edwards Frederick, 4 Okefield terrace, North street
Finch Rev. James (Wesleyan Methodist), New road
Francken William Augustus, Hillside, Station road
Fugler James, Rockleigh
Fulford George Langdon, Highfield
Fulton Mrs. 1 Clarendon villa, New rd
Futcher Chas. Jn. Fairfield, Station rd
Geen Charles J.P. Hill side, Station rd
Geen Henry, Bridge house, Fore st
German John, sen. Kempley road
German Wm.Bird,7 Park vils.Station rd
Giles Rev. Arthur Linzee M.A. (vicar of All Saints' & surrogate), The Vicarage
Grant Miss, Beaumont
Grendon John, St. James street
Gunning Mrs. Downside, Parklands
Hamlyn Tom Parker, West street
Hawken Sam, 6 New road
Holley Major-General Edmund Hunt R.A., J.P. Oaklands
Horne Mrs. Monte Rosa
James Thomas, Sharp hill
James Sydenham John, Fore street
Jessop Hubert, Roseville, Kempley rd

Bellett Frederick, 1 Mount Prospect
Besley John William, Moorside
Bradhurst Wm. Bank ho. Fore street
Brealy Robert, The Lees, Station rd

Jessop Thomas, Kempley road
Johnston Rev. John H. Verney B.A. (curate of All Saints'), Monte Rosa
Kennard Thos. 6 Park vils. Station rd
Kerslake Mrs. Emily, Chapel house, New road
Knapman John, New road
Landick Alfred, New road
Landick Mrs. West Bridge house
Lugg Miss, 3 Mount Prospect
Madden John, North street
Marks Mrs. North street
Marle Mrs. Brandis park, Station rd
May Bert, Lynton house, Station road
Millett Rev. Harold WakeM.A.(curate of All Saints'), Sunnyhurst
Mitchell Mrs. West hill, Camp road
Naylor Miss, Beaumont
Newcombe Simon Peter Brendon J.P. Fairview, Station road
Nourse Miss, Church hill
Paddon William, Beechcroft,Station rd
Palmer James, Fair Place terrace
PassmoreRichd.Solonhurst, Station rd
Pearse Mrs. Parklands
Pearse Wm.Burd,3Park vils Station rd
Pennells Walter, Sharp hill
Phillips Rev. Edgehill, Parklands
Potts Francis, Dursmore, Station rd
Powell Charles Reginald Eversden, Uplands
Prickman John Dunning, River side
Ramsay Lt.-Col. Robert Alexander Douglas R.M.A. Okedene,Station rd

Bradley George F. 2 Park villas, Station road
Burd George Vanhouse, East street
Carpenter Charles Sydenham, East st

Puttock Mrs. 4 Brandis park
Richards Henry, Kempley road
Rowse William, Town mills
Saunders Mrs. Parklands
Smale Ernest James, Okenham villas, Church hill
Snell William, East street
Southcombe William Thos. 1 Parklnds
Sparke Mrs. East street
Spry Frederick, Kempley road
Squire Miss, Castle lane
Ward Albany, Kempley road
Webb William, Fair Place terrace
Westcott Thos. Channings,Prospect ho
White Rev. Abraham S. (Wesleyan Methodist), Wykeham house, Kempley road
White Herbert Egerton, Fore street
Whiting Rev. George James (Baptist), Avenue house, Fair Place ter
Williams Mrs. Michael, Brandize
Winter Rev. W. Jessop (Wesleyan Methodist), Kempley road
Winter Rev. William S. D. (Wesleyan Methodist), Kempley road
Wood Thomas Folley, 4 Park villas, Station road
Wyatt Rev. Francis Bullen (Congregational), 4 Mount Prospect
Yeo Richd. 1 Clarendon villa, New rd
Young Edward Herbert M.D. Darley house, Station road
Young Mrs. 2 Mount Prospect

COMMERCIAL.

Allen Welham, painter, East street
Andrews Fred, Plume of Feathers inn ; every accommodation for visitors & tourists ; good stabling, Fore st
Andrews Robert, Star inn, East street
Anstey Henry, Plymouth inn, West street
Baker John, blacksmith, New road
Ball Grace Ann (Mrs.), apartments, 1 Park View terrace
Ball William, builder & decorator, East street
Batchelor William Frederick, Red Lion hotel, Fore st
Bawden Thomas, apartments, 7 New road
Besley John William Int.Arts.Lond. boarding school for boys, Moorside school
Biddick Frank & Son, butchers, 9 St. James' street
Blackmore Henry, draper, Fore street
Blatchford Grace (Mrs.), apartments, Mount view
Boase Grace (Mrs.), girls' day school, Mayville, Station rd
Bourne Sarah (Mrs.), apartments, 3 Park ter. Station rd
Bradhurst Wm. manager Devon & Cornwall Bank,Fore st
Bray A. R. & Co. drapers, Parade
Bray Alice Mary (Mrs.), apartments, Kempley road
Bray Thomas, horse dealer & dairyman, East street
Bray William, nurseryman & fruiterer, West street
Brayley Thomas, George inn, West street
British Workmen's & General Assurance Co. Lim. (John Henry Helmore, agent) ; district office, East street
Brown Albert James, confectioner, West street
Burd, Pearse & Prickman, solicitors, East street
Burd George Vanhouse, solicitors, East street
Burd George Vanhouse L.R.C.P. & L.M.Edin., M.R.C.S. Eng. surgeon, & medical officer & public vaccinator for Okehampton district & medical officer workhouse, Okehampton union, East street
Cann George Dunning M.A., LL.M. solicitor & commissioner for oaths, attends saturdays, Fore street
Channings Thomas Henry, representative of "Western Daily Mercury," Fore street
Chastey George, jun. wheelwright, Drews cottage
Ching George Edwin, draper & aparts. Northfield road
Clarke Charles Thomson, manager Nat. Provincial Bank of England Lim. Parade
Clinick George, boot & shoe maker, North street
Clinnock Thomas, shopkeeper, East street
Cockwill Matilda (Mrs.), butcher, 15 Northfield road
Coles Rhoda (Miss), milliner & dress ma. Fair Place ter
Convalescent Home (Miss Lily Eliza Burgess, hon. supt.), Station road
Coombe James, hair dresser, East street
Cornish John, ironmonger & china dealer, Fore street
Cornish William Henry, watch maker & jeweller, Fore st
County Court (George Langdon Fulford, registrar & high bailiff), Station road
Cowling Edwin, apartments, 7 Parade
Crocker William Henry, tinplate worker,, Rosemary row
Cummins Bessie (Mrs.), apartments, Okement terrace
Davidson William, grocer, Fore street
Dawe Albert, ironmonger, 32 Fore street

Dawe William Henry, stationer, bookseller & fancy repository, 10, 12 & 14 Arcade
Day Thomas & Son, cycle agents, North st. & Arcade
Day Thomas, blacksmith, North street
Devon Constabulary (Noah Parsons & William John Rees, constables), Sharp street
Devon & Cornwall Banking Co. Limited (branch) (Wm. Bradhurst, manager) ; open 10 till 3 ; wed. 10 till 1 ; sat. 10 till 4, Fore street ; draw on Barclay & Co. Lim. London E C
Devon & Exeter Savings Bank (John Dunning Prickman, agent), East street
Dicker John Lethbridge, apartments, 10 Brandis park
Dingley, Pearse & Co. (branch) (Okehampton Bank), bankers ; open 10 till 3 ; wed. till 1 ; sat. till 4, Fore street; draw on the London City & Midland Bank Limited, London E C
Drew & Hain, painters & paperhangers, East street
Drew Henry & Son, shoe makers, West street
Drew John, apartments, Walmer house, North street
Drew William, shoe maker, Cornishes passage, Fore street
Duffy Emma Amelia (Mrs.), boarding & day school for young ladies, Dark House school
Duffy Thomas, wool stapler & seed merchant, Fore street
Dunn & Baker, solicitors & commissioners for oaths, attends saturdays, Fore street ; & at Exeter & Crediton
Dyment James Ware, apartments, 25 East street
Dymond Richard, grocer, East street
Dymond William, Exeter inn, East street
Eades Elizabeth (Mrs.), confectioner, 13 The Arcade
Edgcombe Richard, assistant supt. to Pearl Assurance Co. Limited, New road
Edgcombe & Sons, clothiers & hatters, Fore street & 1 The Arcade
Edwards Frederick, inspector of weights & measures, Tavistock district, East bridge
Ellis Peter, carter, St. James street
Farrant Maria (Mrs.), dress ma. & aprts. Kempley road
Fewins & May, auctioneers, Lynton house, Station road
Ford George, basket maker, North street
Friend Thomas, dining rooms, West street
Friendship John, butcher, Fore street
Fulford George Langdon, solicitor & commissioner for oaths, town clerk, clerk to the Okehampton Rural District Council, registrar & high bailiff of the county court, clerk to the guardians & assessment & school attendance committees of Okehampton union & supt. registrar of Okehampton district, Station road ; & at North Tawton
Furse William, shopkeeper, North street
Gay George Lavis, wheelwright, East street
Gay Marwood, dairyman, 8 The Arcade
Geen Charles, electrical engineer, Hill side, Station road
Geen Harry, architect & civil engineer, 7 Brandis park
Geen Henry, cabinet maker & builder, East bridge

71

The building of the National Provincial Bank in 1910/11. It is now the National Westminster. It cost £2,587 to build.

F. Tucker & Sons, wheelwrights and blacksmiths, also carriage builders of Market Street. Here they are on market day with carts and implements on display.

German John & Sons, boot & shoe factors & leather merchants, Parade; manufactory, Clapps mills
Glass James, agricultural implement maker, Kempley road & Market street
Guest Richard, apartments, 3 Brandis park
Gunn Samuel Pickard, mineral water manufacturer, coal merchant & deputy registrar births & deaths for Okehampton sub-district, Kempley road
Halcombe Sack Co. (John Rampton, agt.), Railway statn
Harris William, mason, 18 North street
Harris William, town crier, North street
Harry Seth, grocer & registrar of marriages for Okehampton district, Fore street
Hawken Sam, accountant, New road
Heywood John George, White Hart family & commercial hotel & posting house; billiards, rooms en suite &c. Parade
Hill Simon, apartments, Parklands
Hoare Isaac, apartments, & collector of borough rates, Station road
Hodge Charles, baker & confectioner, Fore street
Hodge James, apartments, Parklands
Hodge Philip, baker, North street
Holding Emanuel, boot maker, North street
Holmes George, draper & grocer, & agent for W. & A. Gilbey Limited, wine & spirit merchants, London ho. East parade
Horne Sydney, miller (water), corn factor & farmer, Brightley mill & Station street
Hucker Albert, blacksmith, Kempley road
Hucker Charles, butcher, Fore street
Hucker Jane (Mrs.), blacksmith, St. James street
Hunt William Nettleship, purveyor of farm produce, Northfield road
Hutchings John & Son, confectioners & grocers, West st
Hutchings Ann (Mrs.), apartments, East street
Jackson John Hadwen, chemist, 15 Arcade
James George, Fountain hotel & grazier, Commercial hotel ; posting in all its branches, East street
James Sydenham John & Ada (Miss), printers & stationers, Fore street & 2 Arcade
James Sydenham John, organist at All Saints' church, Fore street
Jessop Thomas, insurance agent & deputy registrar of marriages, Okehampton district, Kempley road
Kemp Richard, tailor, West street
Kerslake William, coal dealer, Sharp hill
King's Arms Hotel (Albert Edwin Guy, proprietor) ; good stabling, lock-up coach houses; break parties catered for ; landaus, waggonettes, dog-carts & saddle horses always on hire at moderate charges; all orders by post receive prompt & personal attention, St. James' street
Landick Alfred, solicitor, New road
Landick Laura (Mrs.), tanner & boot maker, Westbridge
Landick Samuel, jun. apartments, New road
Leach Samuel, cowkeeper, East street
Lee Elizabeth Jane (Mrs.), grocer, St. James street
Literary Institution (Herbert Egerton White, sec. ; Wm. Burd Pearse, treasurer), Town hall
Lucas John Archibald P.A.S.I. architect, attends saturdays, St. James street
Lugg Thomas James, watch maker & photographer, 3 The Arcade
Maddaford Sophia (Mrs.), baker, Northfield road
Marks Robert Melluish, baker & confectioner, Fore street
Marle Alice Fowler (Mrs.), boarding school, Brandis park. See advertisement
Masonic Hall (Lodge Obedience, No. 1573 ; Frederick Edwards, sec.), Station road
May & Son, auctioneers & house & estate agents, Lynton house, Station road ; & at Crediton
May Bert, auctioneer, see May & Son
Medland Elizabeth (Mrs.), apartments, Greystone, Station road
Medland Moses, lessee of market tolls & thatcher, East st
Meecham Sarah (Mrs.), temperance hotel ; every accommodation for tourists & commercial gentlemen; head quarters of the cyclists' touring club, Fore street (adjoining the post office)
Mitchell Ivan, apartments, Parklands
Mitchell Martha (Mrs.), aparts. West hill, Camp road
Mudge William, apartments, 3 Park View terrace
Murrin Emanuel, miller (water), North street
National Provincial Bank of England Limited (branch) ; open to till 3 ; wed. to till 1 ; sat. to till 4 (Charles Thomson Clarke, manager), Parade ; draw on head office, 112 Bishopsgate within, London E C
Newcombe E. & Sons, grocers, wine & spirit & general merchants, West street
Nicholls George Henry, boot maker, East street
Okehampton Bank, see Dingley, Pearse & Co

Watkins William, butcher, East street
Weaver Reginald John, hair dressr. & tobcenst. 11 Arcade
Webb William, hair dresser, Fore street
Weekes Thomas, saddler, Fore street
Westcott Thomas Chamings & Co.drapers & grocrs.Fore st
Wilkinsons Caterers Lim. Pretoria wine stores, North st
Wood Brothers, manure manufacturers
Wood Henry, apartments, 7 Northfield road
Wooldridge Alice (Mrs.), milliner & dress ma. North st
Worden Emanuel, cabinet maker, West street
Worden Francis James, borough surveyor & sanitary inspector, Town hall

Okehampton Agricultural Association (Charles Reginald Evernden Powell, sec.), Town hall
Okehampton Free General Society (Charles Sprague. sec.), Town hall
Okehampton Gas Co. Lim. (Frederick Edwards, sec.), 1 Oakton rest, North street
Okehampton Tradesmen's Friendly Society (Charles Sprague, sec.), Town hall
Oliver Arthur Llewellyn, insurance agent & apartments, Parklands
Osborne Frederick John, confectioner, St. James street
Palmer's Temperance Hotel (William Palmer, proprietor), family hotel, restaurant & lodging house, conveniently situated ; every comfort ; strictly moderate charges, opposite Arcade entrance, Station road
Parker Bartholomew, saddler, Fore street
Passmore Richard, coal merchant & carrier, & agent for the South Western Railway Co. Station road
Pease Thomas Henry Ormiston, solicitor, East street
Penberthy Richard, builder & farmer, Northcott cottage
Pengelly Henry, dairyman, 3 North street
Pengelly John, shopkeeper, West street
Perkin William Edward, corn & seed merchant, Market street ; & at Tavistock
Perkins John Easton, insurance agent, North street
Perkins Mark, cowkeeper, North street
Phear Mary Jane (Mrs.), sports. Ferndale, Station road
Phillips Daniel, draper, East bridge
Powlesland William, cowkeeper, 4 St. James street
Prickman John Dunning (firm, Burd, Pearse & Prickman), solicitor, commissioner for oaths & perpetual commissioner, coroner for Devon (Okehampton district), clerk to county & borough magistrates, the South Tawton & Inwardleigh school boards & agent for Devon & Exeter Savings Bank, East street
Pyke, Powlesland & Son, auctioneers, land agents & surveyors (attend saturdays), West street ; & at Bow & North Tawton
Quance John, farmer, East street & Alforden
Rich Alfred, travelling draper, Moor view, North street
Rich Richard, blacksmith, East street
Rich William Hy. fruiterer & florist, 4 & 7 Arcade
Richards Henry, grocer 6, & draper 5, The Arcade
Rogers William John, tailor, St. James street
Rowe Henry, travelling draper, Kempley road
Rowe William Selway, butcher & poulterer, East street
Rowse William, miller (water), corn merchant & farmer, Town mills & Yelland farm ; & at Cleve mill, Sticklepath, Belstone
Seldon John, shoe maker, St. James street
Shipman Sidney, apartments, 1 Park terrace, Station rd
Sleo George, farmer, Northfield road
Sleeman John James, builder & joiner, Kempley road
Smale Bessie Beatrice (Mrs.), fruiterer, Fore street
Smale George, sanitary inspector to the Okehampton Rural District Council, North street
Smith W. H. & Son, booksellers & news agents, Railway station
Southcombe William Thomas, inland revenue officer, 9 Parklands
Sparke James, butcher, Parade
Spiers & Pond Lim. refreshment rooms, Railway station
Sprague Charles, stationer & assistant overseer, collector of taxes & poor's rates & clerk to the school board, West street
Spreadborough Walter, apartments, 3 Parklands
Spry Frederick, accountant, registrar of births & deaths & vaccination officer for Okehampton sub-district & relieving & school attendance officer No. 2 district, Okehampton union & borough auditor, Kempley road
Stanbury John, apartments, 1 Brandis park
Stenning & Hanniford (Misses), milliners, 9 The Arcade
Stincheombe Edward, watch maker & jeweller, Fore street
Stone John, apartments, Dartmoor house, Station road
Stone Philip, china dealer, St. James street
Stoneman Richard, apartments, Mount view
Stratford Alice (Miss), apartments, East street
Tardrew Emily & Eliza (Misses), boarding ho. Parklands
Thorburn Edwin John M.R.C.V.S. vet. surgn. Station rd
Toms James Gray, London hotel, West street
Town Hall (Alfred John Metherell, keeper), Fore street
Treble William, tailor, East street
Tregunna Thomas Morris, supt. to the Prudential Assurance Co. East street
Tucker Francis Geo. poulterer & fruiterer, 14 The Arcade
Vaughan Charles, teacher of music & organist of South Tawton church, Beulah, Station road
Volunteer Battalion (4th) Devonshire Regiment (D Co. ; (Capt. & Hon. Major H. C. Biddell V.D.), Drill Hall, The Market hall
Ward William Thos. & Sons, carriage bldrs. Station road
Ward & Co. (branch), coal & lime mers. Railway station

Workmen's Club (Mrs. W. H. Holley, president ; F. J. Warden, sec ; Herbert E. White, treas.), St. James st
Wright James, china dealer & ironmonger, Fore street
Yelland John, grocer, Northfield road
Yeo Eliza (Mrs.), tailoress, West street
Yeo Isaac, tailor, dairyman & insurance agent, Fore st
Yeo William Henry, printer, West street
Youldon John, apartments, 2 Brandis park
Young Edward Herbert M.D.Durh., D.P.H.Lond., M.R.C.S.Eng. surgeon & medical officer of health, Okehampton borough & Rural District Council, Darley ho. Station road

Squire's stationery shop, and Tolley the saddlers. The placards read 'Flying Man in Exeter today' and 'The King's Adventures in the zoo'.

The Bus House, Okehampton.

Rosemary Row.

The Arcade.

PARKHAM is a parish and village on the small river Yeo, and is bounded on the north by Barnstaple Bay, 7 miles south-west from Bideford station on the Torrington branch of the London and South Western railway, in the North Western division of the county, Shebbear hundred, Bideford petty sessional division, union and county court district, rural deanery of Hartland, archdeaconry of Barnstaple and diocese of Exeter. The church of St. James is an edifice of stone of the 15th century, consisting of chancel, nave, aisles, south porch and an embattled western tower, of Perpendicular date, with pinnacles and containing 6 bells, all cast in 1778: there are four stained windows, an enriched Norman door and a font of the same period: the north aisle was erected by the Risdon family, of Bableigh, in this parish, and in the aisle is a slab inscribed on one side to Giles Risdon, gent. ob. 21st April, 1583, æt. 90, and on the other to Grace, wife of Giles Risdon, of Bableigh, ob. 10th February, 1676, and Katherine, wife of the same, ob. 11th September, 1682: there are also various inscriptions from 1595 to 1712, to the ancient family of Giffard, of Halsbury, ancestors of present Lord Halsbury, Lord Chancellor, 1885-92; one of these is on a stone bearing on the proper obverse side an inscription to Katherine, wife of Thomas Moncke, of Pudderydge esq. ob. 2nd November, 1595: in the south aisle is a flat stone with an enriched margin and incised floriated cross, surrounded by an inscription in old English lettering to Richard——, ob. 14-6: the church was restored in 1875, and has 250 sittings. The register dates from the year 1538. The living is a rectory, net yearly income £500, inclusive of 127 acres of glebe, with residence, in the gift of and held since 1889 by the Rev. Robert William John Smart M.A. of Queen's College, Oxford. There are two Wesleyan chapels, one in the village and one at Holwell, and a Bible Christian chapel at Goldworthy, one mile distant. The Barton of Halsbury, from which the present Lord Chancellor derives his title, went from the family of that name to the Giffards by marriage in the reign of Edward I. Halsbury now belongs to T. Rogers esq. by purchase from the Lees, who bought it of the Davies family, to whom the Giffards sold it. Bableigh, once a residence of the Risdons, was sold in 1760 to Mr. Hiern. One-third of the manor belongs to the Hon. Mark G. K. Rolle, of Stevenstone; another third, once in the Molesworths, has been sold in parcels. The Hon. Mark George Kerr Rolle, Trehawke Kekewich esq. of Peamore, Exeter; Major James Morrison Kirkwood, of Yeo Vale, Alvington, Bideford; Mrs. Pine-Coffin, of Portledge and Kenwith, Abbotsham, Bideford; and Thomas Rogers esq. of Orleigh Court, Buckland Brewer, Bideford, are the chief landowners. The soil is various; subsoil, clay. The land is chiefly in pasturage. The area is 5,924 acres of land and 92 of foreshore; rateable value, 3,291; the population in the civil parish in 1901 was 797.

By Local Government Board Order 14,829, detached parts of Buckland Brewer, known as Howley and Green Hill, were added to this parish, March 25, 1885, for civil purposes.

An unknown family group, possibly the Able family, posing at Bocombe Bridge. Note the straw-covered beehives in the background.

PARKHAM.

Coombe Miss
Dunkerton Mrs. Hoops
Pitcairn Mrs. South Yeo
Smart Rev.Rt. Wm.Jn. M.A. Rectory

COMMERCIAL.

Abel William P.(Mrs.),farmer,Bocombe
Andrew George, farmer, Barton
Andrew John, farmer, Linches
Andrew John, farmer, Flaxmans
Andrew William, farmer, Limebury
Arnold Thomas, Bell inn, blacksmith & farmer
Becklake William, farmer, Holwell
Becklake William, farmer, Sloo
Blight Daniel, tailor & grocer
Broom George, butcher
Burrow William Davey, relieving officer Western district & registrar of births, deaths & marriages & vaccination officer for Hartland sub-district, Bideford union, Hill view, Hoops
Clements Anthony & Son, builders, Bocombe
Cleverdon Wm. farmer, Tucking mill
Durant Thomas, farmer & miller (water), Bocombe mill
Emtage Edmund Walter M.R.C.S. Eng. surgeon, & medical officer & public vaccinator, No. 1 district, Holsworthy union & Parkham district, Bideford union; & at Cleverdon house, Bradworthy

Folland Thomas H. deputy registrar of births & deaths, Parkham sub-district, Bideford union
George Arthur, farmer, Cabbacott
George Giles, farmer, Cabbacott
Goaman Richard, farmer, Waytown
Grigg Seth, farmer, Babeleigh
Heddon John,farmer, Halsbury Barton
Heywood George, farmer, Watershut
Heywood John, farmer, Lower Worthygate
Heywood Joseph, farmer, Bowden
Heywood Thomas, farmer, Steart
Hutchings Susan (Mrs.), dress maker
Jewell John Thomas, farmer, Culver Park villa
Lane Thomas, builder, Newhaven
Lang Thomas, Hoop's inn & farmer
Martin Frederick, shoe maker, registrar of births & deaths, Parkham sub-district, Bideford union & clerk to the school board & attendance officer & assistant overseer
Moore Richard, farmer, Moor farm
Mugford Charles, farmer, Bank hole
Parr Charles, farmer & machinist
Pearce Wm. miller (water), Old mill
Pennington James, sanitary inspector, Bideford rural district council
Petherick Dl. farmer, Higher Waytwn
Pridham Daniel, farmer & road contractor, Hoar hill
Sanders Thomas & Sons, farmers & bakers, Kerswell

Slee Wm. Bryant, farmer, Sedboro'
Squire Ernest John, plumber, painter & farmer, Northway
Squire Frederick Charles, boot maker
Turner George, farmer, Nethercott
Turner John, farmer & surveyor to the Bideford rural district council, Northway
Walter Richard, farmer & carpenter, New road

ASH.

Honey John, farmer
Norman Henry Newcombe, farmer

BROAD PARKHAM.

Goaman Richard, farmer
Harding Albert John, farmer
Lang Caleb, farmer & cattle dealer

GOLDWORTHY.

Ford Robt. farmer, East Goldworthy
Grigg Seth, farmer, West Goldworthy
Grigg Wm. farmer, East Goldworthy
Vaggers Reuben, mason & farmer

HORNSCROSS.

Allin Caroline (Mrs.), shopkeeper
Clement John, oilman
Jenkins John T. Coach & Horses P.H
Jenkins William, farmer & carpenter
Peard John, blacksmith
Walter Sydney, carpenter

ASH, about 2 miles south-west ; BROAD PARKHAM, 1½ miles north-west ; BUCKISH MILLS, 3 miles northwest on the sea coast ; GOLDWORTHY, 1 mile northeast, where the ancestors of the poet Gay resided and HORNSCROSS, 1½ miles north, are hamlets.

Post Office, Parkham.—Mrs. Mary Elizabeth Martin, subpostmistress. Letters received from Bideford at 9.20 a.m. ; dispatched at 4.45 p.m. ; sundays, received at 9.10 a.m. ; dispatched at 9.20 a.m. Postal orders are issued here, but not paid. Bideford is the nearest money order office & Hornscross, 2 miles distant, the nearest telegraph office

Post & T. O. & Express Delivery Office, Hornscross.— Thomas James, sub-postmaster. Letters received from Bideford at 8.20 a.m. ; dispatched at 5.46 p.m. ; sundays, dispatched at 4.46 p.m. Postal orders are issued here, but not paid. The nearest money order office is at Bideford

Schools.

A School Board of 5 members was formed April 12, 1873 ; Frederick Martin, clerk to the board & attendance officer

Board (mixed), erected in 1863, for 130 children ; average attendance, 87 ; Thomas Henry Folland, master ; Mrs. Folland, sewing mistress

Board, Hoops (infants), erected in 1876, for 50 children ; average attendance, 38 ; Mrs. Rosa Harding, mistress

PETROCKSTOW (or Stow St. Petrock) is a parish and village, on the road from Hatherleigh to Torrington, 7½ miles south-by-east from Torrington station on a branch of the London and South Western railway and 4½ north-north west from Hatherleigh, and in the Northern division of the county, Shebbear hundred, Torrington petty sessional division, union and county court district, rural deanery of Torrington, archdeaconry of Barnstaple and diocese of Exeter. The church of St. Petrock is a building of stone in the Perpendicular style, consisting of chancel, nave of three bays, aisles, south porch and an embattled western tower with pinnacles, containing 5 bells: there are several monuments to the Rolle and other families, including a brass to Henry, 4th son of George Rolle esq. of Stevenstone, and his wife, Margaret (Yeo), ob. 1591, with kneeling effigies of both and of their ten sons and nine daughters, shields of arms and inscriptions: the carved oak reredos, erected in 1886, is a memorial: in 1888 a window was placed to Mr. Moase, formerly of Petrockstow, who died in America; there is another erected in 1891 to Louis Woollcombe M.A. rector, 1845-83, d. 1889, and one to his widow and daughter, 1895; the font is Norman, but has a cover of Perpendicular date: in 1895 an organ was provided at a cost of £120: the church was entirely rebuilt, with the exception of the tower, in 1879-80 at a cost of upwards of £2,000, and in 1887 the tower was re-roofed and repaired throughout, under the direction of Mr. Hooper, of Hatherleigh, at a cost of £600: the church has 250 sittings: the churchyard was laid out, fenced and planted in 1887. The register dates from the

Villagers in Petrockstowe.

year 1597. The living is a rectory, net yearly value £174, including 45 acres of glebe, with residence, in the gift of Lord Clinton, and held since 1884 by the Rev. Ernest Walter Field M.A. of Oriel College, Oxford, who is also rural dean of Torrington, and chaplain to Lord Clinton. There is a Wesleyan chapel. The ancient manor house was burnt down many years ago, and the present handsome mansion, called "Heanton Satchville," which stands in the adjoining parish of Huish is the seat of Lord Clinton M.A., J.P.; the old house was for some time the seat of the Rolles and the Walpoles, Earls of Oxford. Lord Clinton is lord of the manor and principal landowner; Wood house is the property of Samuel Bonifant esq. The soil is dun kind; the subsoil is clay. The chief crops are wheat, barley, oats and roots. The acreage is 4,288, including 210 acres of woodland, 136 acres of open marsh and the deer park of Heanton Satchville, 136 acres; rateable value, £2,740; the population in 1901 was 384.

Sexton, Joseph Luxton.

Post Office.—William Trace, sub-postmaster. Letters by mail cart through Dolton R.S.O. North Devon, received at 8.15 a.m.; dispatched at 5.20 p.m.; no delivery on sundays. Postal orders are issued here, but not paid. The nearest money order & telegraph office is at Merton, 3 miles distant

Devon Constabulary, Walter Norrish, constable

National School (mixed), built by Lord Clinton in 1842, at a cost of about £700, for 106 children; average attendance, 54; William Britton Edwards, master & Mrs. Isabella Edwards, sewing mistress

Wesleyan Sunday school outing, 20 July 1909.

A family group. Both the family and cottage names would be appreciated, please.

The Lodge.

Field Rev. Ernest Walter M.A.(rector & rural dean), Rectory
Mills John, Wood Turn

COMMERCIAL.

Adams George & Charles, tanners, Quarry hill
Blackmore Wm.frmr.Brightmanshayes
Bridgman John, farmer, North town
Brooks Thomas, farmer, Town farm
Bussell John Geo. farmer, Ash Barton
Cleverdon Thomas, farmer, Westacott
Clinton's (Lord) Brick & Tile Works (Wm. Hunkin, foreman), Berry mr
Davey John, farmer, Stockhey
Dufty John, farmer & nurseryman, Hele Barton

Edwards Ellen (Mrs.), shopkeeper
Ford John, farmer, Thorns
Hatherley Arthur, carpenter & wheelwright, Ash
Headen Fanny (Mrs.),frmr.Netherton
Hockin Francis, farmer, Zeal
Hunkin James, farmer, Woodhouse
Langdon Edwin, auctioneer & valuer & agent for Westminster Fire, Rose cottage
Leonard Mrs.frmr.Denfords, Sincock
Letheren George, farmer, Sincock
Martin John, farmer, Little Marland
Mills William, farmer, Foxhill
Moore Francis, farmer, Hook
Petherick Ann (Mrs.), farmer, Berry
Pickard John, farmer, Allisland

Quance Mary (Mrs.), farmer, Hall
Ridge Robert, registered shoeing & general smith & agricultural implement maker & agent, Brandis hl
Saunders Isaac, chimney swpr. Hall
Sillifant Elizabeth (Mrs.), shopkeepr
Slade Thomas, farmer, Chilsdon
Squance James, jun. farmer, Heanton Barton
Steer Richard, farmer, Butstone
Stevens William, farmer, South hill
Trace Edwin, insurance agent
Trace Wm. boot & shoe ma. Post off
Tucker Titus, wheelwright & farmer, Stockhey
Ward Ann (Mrs.), farmer, Hallwood

The primary school, Petrockstowe, now demolished.

Northtown. John Bridgeman was the farmer there in 1902.

PETERS MARLAND is a parish and village, on the high road from Torrington to Hatherleigh, 6 miles south from Torrington station of a branch of the London and South Western railway and 12½ south from Bideford, in the Northern division of the county, Shebbear hundred, Torrington petty sessional division, union and county court district, rural deanery of Torrington, archdeaconry of Barnstaple and diocese of Exeter. The church of St. Peter, rebuilt in 1865, at the sole expense of J. C. Moore-Stevens esq. is a building of stone, in the Early English style, consisting of chancel, nave, aisles, south porch and an embattled western tower with pinnacles containing 5 bells, of which the first is dated 1664; the 2nd, 1759; the 3rd has an inscription in Old English letters; the 4th a prayer to the Virgin in Lombardic capitals; the tenor was cast by Warner, of London, in 1865, when the whole peal was re-hung: some old brasses remain: the stained east window is a memorial to the Ven. J. Moore-Stevens, Archdeacon of Exeter, who died in 1865, and was placed by his son, J. C. Moore-Stevens esq. of Winscott, who also erected two other windows in memory of his children: the church was restored in 1875-91 at a cost of £920, and affords 150 sittings. There is a lych gate on the south side of the churchyard. The register of baptisms and burials dates from the year 1696; marriages, 1697. The living is a vicarage, yearly value £46, with residence and 15 acres of glebe, in the gift of J. C. Moore-Stevens esq. A Bible Christian chapel was erected in 1870. Cleveland's charity amounts to £5 yearly and a farm producing about £31 yearly. Here are the works of the North Devon Clay Co. Limited, of Torrington; the products of these works are conveyed to Torrington by a tram line seven miles in length and in direct communication with the L. and S. W. railway. The manor was at an early period in the family of Marshall (ancestors of J. P. Sydenham Marshall esq. of Barnstaple), from which it passed to the Northcotes (Earls of Iddesleigh) and Arvingtons, who also owned Little Dunsford in this county. Twigbear is the only manor now known here, and it belongs to E. J. Oldham esq. of Hatherleigh. John Curzon Moore-Stevens esq. D.L., J.P. is the owner of and resides at Winscott, and is also impropriator of the great tithes, which formerly belonged to the priory of Frithelstock. The land is all freehold. E. J. Oldham esq. J. C. Moore-Stevens esq. The Misses Wren, of Lenwood, Bideford and Lord Clinton are chief landowners. The soil is various; the subsoil is clay and rock. The chief crops are wheat, barley and oats. The area is 2,538 acres; rateable value, £1,746; the population in 1901 was 297.

By Local Government Board Order, 14,971, Alscott was transferred from Langtree to this parish, March 24, 1884.

Post, M. O. O., S. B. & Annuity & Insurance Office.—John Mitchell, sub-postmaster. Letters through Torrington, which is the nearest telegraph office, arrive at 9.40 a.m.; dispatched at 4.35 p.m. Wall Letter Boxes, near the church, cleared at 4.15 p.m.; & near Yard cottages at 4.55 p.m. week days only

School (mixed), built in 1872, for 80 children; average attendance, 45; Mrs. C. E. Drinkwater, mistress; & supported at the sole expense of J. C. Moore-Stevens esq

The post office. John Mitchell was listed as draper and grocer, as well as sub-postmaster, in 1902. The building still looks the same today.

South View, Winscott. The big window cost £100 to install. The whole building has now been demolished.

Eastwood Cottages.

Claymore Cottages, these are made of white Marland brick.

East Yard, Peters Marland. Included here is an extract from *Strong's Industries of North Devon*.

'It is a pleasant drive, encircling the wooded hills, and rising to heights commanding extensive views of a fair country, that takes us from the Torrington terminus of the London and South Western Railway to the Marland Terra Cotta and Brick Works. A light railway line, six miles in extent, exists for the conveyance of clay and the manufacturers of the Marland Works to the South Western Company's Station. Through a famous hunting country of which the Gribble Inn, a popular "meet", is the centre, we run to Yarde, a little hamlet less than a mile from the works, where a foreman's residence and sixteen workmen's cottages – built of course of Marland brick – have been erected for the accommodation of the employees. Between Yarde and Clay Moor we pass Winscott, the pleasant residence of J.C.Moore-Stevens, Esq., that stands on a wooded eminence which overlook the extensive property of the Squire.'

Moore-Stevens John Curzon D.L., J.P. Winscott
Balkwill John, farmer
Balkwill Mary Copp (Mrs.), farmer, West yard
Curtice Henry, farmer, Coombe
Dunn Jesse, farmer, Alscott (letters should be addressed Shebbear, Highampton)
Ellis Charles Henry, farmer, Eastwd

Folland Frederick, farmer, Stone
Hearn Wm. farmer, Week Barton
Hooper Rowland, farm bailiff to J. C. Moore-Stevens esq. Winscott
Hurkin George, farmer, Twigbear
Hutchins John, blacksmith
Marland Brick Works (proprietors, The North Devon Clay Co. Lim.) (Henry Holwill, manager); office, Torrington

Mills Jesse, boot & shoe maker
MitchellJn,draper & grocer,Post office
North Devon Clay Company Limited (Henry Holwill, manager); office, Torrington
Quance Samuel, blacksmith
Slade John, farmer, Stone
Tanton John, farmer, Buda
Watkins William, farmer, Wollaton

A train on the Torrington and Marland Light Railway Line. It was a 3 ft gauge line, opened in 1880 exclusively for the clayworks, but it also carried other merchandise to help pay for its upkeep. Here the train is crossing a timber viaduct.

A train at Peters Marland pithead. This line was superseded in 1925 by the Torrington to Halwill line of the Southern Railway Co. and was closed down in the 1960s.

The stacks and kilns of the clay pits, *c.* 1900.

These trucks were probably full of brickbats and other waste material which was ground down and used again in the production of terracotta.

The big pit at the clayworks. Until 1930 the clay was all worked with hand tools – a wedge-like spade, and an adze-like implement called a bale. The bales of clay weighed about 18 lbs each; this photograph was taken between 1930 and 1940.

Men working for the North Devon Clay Company. It looks as though mechanical drills and shovels were being used by them. This was also probably c. 1935.

A portrait of two clayworkers, J. Poole and F. Ebsworthy, c. 1932.

RIDDLECOMBE is a hamlet 1½ miles north-west from the village. Messrs. J. M. and R. G. Harris are lords of the manor.

Post Office, Riddlecombe.—Samuel Boundy, sub-postmaster. Letters through Chulmleigh arrive at 8.45 a.m.; dispatched 5.10 p.m. Postal orders are issued here, but not paid. Dolton is the nearest money order & telegraph office, 3 miles distant

National School (mixed), erected in 1861 & endowed with £45 by Mrs. Pyncombe, for 100 children; average attendance, 59; James Shopland, master; Miss Alice Owen, assistant mistress

Laura Harris, c. 1906. Note the Prudential notice on the door.

Richard Harris possibly home on leave during the First World War?

Outside the blacksmiths, c. 1906. From left to right: -?-, Mr Bagley, Jim Boundy, Mary Alford, Florence Ockridge, John Greenslade and Susan Boundy who kept the shop in the background, and married Bill Chamber, the grocer at Winkleigh.

RIDDLECOMBE.

Alford Robert, shoe maker
Boundy Samuel, tailor, outfitter & grocer, Post office
Carter Geo. & Jas. farmers, Knaplocks
Carter John & Son, carpenters & shop-keepers
Greenslade John, blacksmith
Harris Robert & Sons, farmers, Riddle-combe Hole, Skellies & Hayes farms
Harris Jonathan, carpenter & wheel-wright
Harris William, farmer, Chichester
Parker Robert, mason
Parkhouse William, farmer
Western Joseph, carrier

ROBOROUGH is a parish and village, 4½ miles south-west from Portsmouth Arms station on the North Devon branch of the London and South Western railway, 6 east from Torrington and 10 south-east from Bideford, in the Northern division of the county, Fremington hundred, Torrington petty sessional division, union and county court district, and in the rural deanery of Torrington, archdeaconry of Barnstaple and diocese of Exeter. The church of St. Peter is an edifice of stone in the Early English style, consisting of chancel, nave, south aisle, south porch and an embattled western tower, with pinnacles, containing 6 bells; the old tenor bell, weighing 14 cwts. 2 qrs. was given by Roger Wollacombe esq. in 1706, but the whole peal was re-cast by W. and J. Taylor, of Oxford, in 1823, from the previous peal of 5 bells: in the chancel is a stained window, inserted by the late rector in 1868 to the memory of his parents: the church was restored in 1868 and has 220 sittings. The register dates from the year 1619. The living is a rectory, net yearly value £220, including 56 acres of glebe, with residence, in the gift of Mrs. E. W. May, and held since 1897 by the Rev. Edward Henry Fox May B.A. of Turrell's Hall, Oxford. Here is a Wesleyan chapel. Ebberly House, the residence of Thomas Batson esq. J.P. is a

The village.

handsome modern building, pleasantly situated. The lord of the manor and the Hon. Mark George Kerr Rolle are the chief landowners. The soil is clayey; subsoil, stone. The chief crops are cereal. The area is 3,212 acres; rateable value, £2,170; the population in 1901 was 312.

Post Office.—Edwin Pincombe, sub-postmaster. Letters arrive at 10 a.m. from Beaford R.S.O. ; dispatched at 4.10 p.m. Postal orders are issued here, but not paid. Beaford is the nearest money order office & telegraph office, 3 miles distant

Public Elementary School (mixed), built in 1854 & enlarged in 1872, for 90 children; average attendance, 67; & supported in part by a legacy of £250 bequeathed by Miss Maria Horndon in 1858; the managers are the rector & churchwardens; Walter Pritchard, master

Batson Thomas J.P. Ebberly house
May Rev. Edward Henry Fox B.A. Rectory

COMMERCIAL.

Allin Thomas, farmer, Cliston
Badcock James, farmer, Coombe
Bealey Eli, farmer, Villavin
Bealey Richard, blacksmith
Bealey John, farmer, Newcombs
Blackmore Hy. farmer, Cawsey's farm
Clemens Hy. farmer, Low. Barlington
Featherstone William, miller (water) & farmer, Owlacombe mill

Folland Thomas, farmer, Sugworthy
Friend Arthur, mason
Hopper Jn.butcher & frmr.Ea.Rapson
Isaac William, shoe maker
Lemon Ann & Mary J. (Misses), farmers, Villavin
Martin Grace (Mrs.), baker
Maynard John Bealey, New inn & farmer
Maynard Jonathan, shoe maker
Pardon John, carpenter
Pardon Lewis, carpenter
Pincombe Edwin, shoe ma. Post office
Price Robert Wm. frmr. Owlacombe

Prouse Robert, farmer, Thelbridge
Reed John, farmer, Parkins
Reed Thomas R. farmer & assistant overseer, Parkins
Richards Thomas, farmer, Rapson
Rockey William, wheelwright
Squire Fras. frmr. Gt. & Lit.Wansley
Squire Henry, mason
Squire John, farmer, Handfords
Squire Thomas,farmer, Gt. Barlington
Thomas Julian A. frmr. Ebberley frm
Turner Edith (Miss), shopkeeper
Ward Wm. miller (water),Coombe ml

A house at Roborough.

The schoolchildren in Roborough.

Miss Florrie Featherstone at the door of Owlacombe Mill.

The New Inn. It was closed for several years and was now re-opened and is flourishing.

A view of the church.

The wheelbarrow race, sports day 1909. The gentleman with white sideburns (sixth from right) is Jo Elliot the photographer, in a photograph taken by his son.

The view looking south. In the garden of the pub is Mrs Maynard (left) and her sister. The Maynards were farmers and innkeepers. In the foreground is Mr Waldron, a thatcher.

Devon County Dairy School, 1907. The photograph was taken outside the door of the New Inn. Back row: John Maynard, and possibly Mr Waldron. In the top row there is a Miss Page and Bessy Bright is third from the right. In the second row, Jessy Badcock is fourth from the left and Lucy Badcock is third from the right. In the bottom row, far right, is Elizabeth Ann Squance, the little boy is Roy Maynard.

SAMPFORD COURTENAY is a parish and village, near the road from Crediton to Okehampton, with a station 2 miles south-east of the village, on the main line of the London and South Western railway, and is 5 miles north-north-east from Okehampton and 194 from London, in the Western division of the county, Black Torrington hundred, Hatherleigh petty sessional division, Okehampton union and county court district, rural deanery of Okehampton, archdeaconry of Totnes and diocese of Exeter. The village is supplied with water for drinking purposes from Ladywell spring, the water being conveyed through pipes laid down in 1887 at a cost of £50. Under the provisions of the "Local Government Act, 1894," the adjoining parish of Honeychurch was added to this parish for all purposes except ecclesiastical. The church of St. Andrew is an ancient building of stone in the Perpendicular style, consisting of chancel, nave, aisles with arcades of five arches, south porch and a lofty embattled western tower, with pinnacles, containing a clock and 6 bells, all cast in 1770: the fine carved oak roof, at present almost entirely hidden by plastering, displays two carved bosses, with busts representing an earl and countess of the Courtenay family of the 14th century: two others bear the figure of a boar and the arms of Courtenay: the rood screen was taken down in 1831, and no remains now exist: the church was restored in 1899 at a cost of £2,500, and affords 300 sittings. The register dates from the year 1558. The living is a rectory, with the chapelry of Sticklepath annexed, net yearly value £389, with residence and about 85 acres of glebe, in the gift of King's College, Cambridge, and held since 1893 by the Rev. Thomas Wright Little M.A. of King's College, Cambridge. There is a chapel for Bible Christians. The charities amount to £2 8s. yearly. Near the Board School is an ancient cross in a good state of preservation; and there are others in different parts

A view of the church entrance. The Prayer Book Rebellion of 1549 is said to have started in this building.

The New Inn, kept by Samuel Hill, a farmer in 1902.

SAMPFORD COURTENAY.

(Marked thus † should be addressed Exbourne R.S.O.)

(Marked thus ‡ should be addressed Okehampton.)

(Marked thus * should be addressed Sticklepath, Okehampton.)

Cross Thomas, Thornberry cottage
Kelland Robert, Yondhill
LittleRev.ThomasWright M.A.Rectory
‡Westaway William, Corscombe

COMMERCIAL.

‡Amery Jn.Westaway,frmr. Corscmbe
Ansty John, farmer, East Rowden
Arscott Hy. school attendance officer
Arscott James Fewing, thrashing machine owner
Arscott William, farmer, Trecott
Arscott William, farmer, West Trecott
Ash Wm. & Sons, builders & contrctrs
Bailey Thomas, farmer, Honeycott
Blanchford Henry (Mrs.), & Son, farmers, Page farm
Bolt Charles, farmer, Langmead
Bolt Emma (Mrs.) & Son, farmers, Fullaford
Brealey Richard, Chapel inn & wheelwright
‡Brock John, farmer, Restland
‡Chasty George, wheelwright
†Coombe James, farmr. MiddleClissn
Coombe Henry, butcher
Dart Thomas Luxton, sen. frmr.Incott
Davey John, farmer, Higher Rowden
†Dayment Elizabeth Ann (Miss), farmer, Higher Clisson
Dayment Elizh. (Miss),frmr.Frankland
Down Jn. Thos. frmr. Corscombe dwn
*Drew Henry Vivian, farmer, Holford

Fewings Robert, shopkeeper, Post off
Finch Isaac, blacksmith
Frost Albert, farmer, West hill
†Hawkins John Edwin, farmer,Solland
Hawkins Robert, farmer, North & South Beer hill
‡Hawkins HenryJohn,farmer,Justmant
Heywood Samuel,frmr.Middle Rowden
Hill Samuel, New inn, & farmer
Holmes William, farmer, Underdown
Hooper George, miller (water) & farmer, Peckets Ford mill
‡Horn William Charles, farmer & assistant overseer, Ball
Kemp Edward,Courtenay Railway inn
‡Knapman William, farmer,Reddaway
Knight Samuel, shoe maker
Lang Wm. & Son, farmers, Barton
‡Newcombe Nicholas, frmr. Webber hl
*Newcombe William, farmer, Lower & Higher Langabeer
*Orchard Thomas, farmer, Willey
*Page John, farmer, Trehill
Parsons William Beer, tailor
Reddaway John, shopkeeper
‡Reddaway William, farmer, Beer
Reed Mary Ann (Mrs.), shopkeeper
Sanders Geo. sen. farmer, Southtown
†Sanders Geo.jun.farmer, Low.Clisson
Sanders Henry Finning, cattle doctor
*Saunders John, farmer, Withybrook
Searle James, farmer, Hatherton
Sloman John, farmer, Lower Rowden
Sloman Thomas, farmer, Middletown, Honeychurch
Snell George, farmer, Middle town
†SnellJn.Huxtable,frmr.Low.Domaford
‡Southcombe Samuel, farmer, Wood
Stanbury Charles, farmer, Lydcott
Stentiford John, shopkeeper

Thomas James Eva, farmer, Hayrish
Ward John Eastabrook,builder,& sub-agent for King's college, Cambridge

STICKLEPATH.

(Letters should be addressed Okehampton.)

Fewins Mrs
Finch Albany George, Cleave house
Finch James, Silverlake
Finch Thomas, Primula house
Rhodes Miss, Millbrook cottage
Wills William, Steedaford

COMMERCIAL.

Ching George (Mrs.), farmer, Coombe
Cook John, farmer, Union cottage
Cooke James & Sons, wheelwrights
Cooke Miriam (Mrs.), apartments
Cooper John, farmer & omnibus própr
Dew Henry, insurance agent
Fewins & May, auctioneers
Finch Bros.edge tool & shovel manufrs
Finch Annie (Miss), shopkeeper
Gilbert Thomas Edward, Taw River hotel; every accommodation for visitors & tourists
Hooper James, farmer, Bude
Reddaway Wm. apartmnts. Laurel cot
Rowe John Henry, Devonshire inn
Trethewey Elizabeth & Ellen (Misses), girls' school, The Retreat
Tucker Aubrey William, shopkeeper
Village Hall & Reading Room (Frank Richards, sec)
Yeo George,butcher & wagonette propr
Yeo John Cann, shoe maker & shopkeeper, Post office
Yeo William Henry, baker

100

The village. Middleton Farmhouse is on the left, Lower Middleton Farmhouse on the right, and Green Cottage in the centre.

Rectory Hill. The ladies in the background are Mrs Cooper (the mother of Becky Horn) and possibly Mrs Stone. The Reddaway sisters are outside the post office. 'Buck' Fewings kept the post office in 1907. Robert Fewings is listed in 1902 as being shopkeeper at the post office.

The old Methodist Chapel with thatched roof. The Barton, the Pound building and the Church House are in the foreground.

A view of the footbridge.

SHEBBEAR is a village and parish near the river Torridge, over which is a bridge of one arch to Milton Damerel, and is 5 miles north from Dunsland Cross station on the Halwill and Bude branch of the London and South Western railway, and 9 north-east from Holsworthy, in the Northern division of the county, hundred of Shebbear, Torrington petty sessional division, union and county court district, rural deanery of Torrington, archdeaconry of Barnstaple and diocese of Exeter. The church of St. Michael is of stone in the Perpendicular style, consisting of chancel, nave, south aisle, south porch and a western tower, with pinnacles, containing 6 bells; the first and sixth were cast in 1863, the others in 1792: the porch has a fine Norman arch and a sun dial: the east window is a memorial to the Rev. Peter Davey Foulkes, vicar here from 1829, erected by public subscription in 1887: under an obtuse arch in the south aisle is a tomb with recumbent sandstone effigy of a female in a flowing robe, mantle and veil, and holding a rosary, her head being supported by angels; the figure (1350-1450) is traditionally said to represent the Lady of Ladford: the church was restored and repewed during 1875-92, at a cost of £1,000, and has 500 sittings. The register dates from the year 1576. The living is a vicarage, net yearly value £130, with residence and 3 acres of glebe, in the gift of the Lord Chancellor, and held since 1901 by the Rev. Thomas Edward Fox, of

. The Bible Christian chapel, built in 1817 and rebuilt in 1841, will seat 400 persons; attached is a burial ground: there is also a Wesleyan chapel at New Inn, erected in 1840, and a Baptist chapel at Caute, built in 1884. The Bible Christian Connexional College, near the village, is a spacious building of stone and brick, and includes a large school room, suitable class rooms and large and well-ventilated dormitories; it was enlarged in 1877 at a cost of £4,000, and again in 1883 at a cost of £2,000, and in 1891 at a further of £1,500, and will now hold 120 scholars, the average number being 110; chemical and physical laboratories, a large gymnasium and two new class rooms were added in 1901, and the electric light has been provided for the whole school; the governor's house adjoins, and there are six resident masters; annexed is a farm of about 100 acres in extent, the gift of the Right Hon. Samuel James Way P.C. Chief Justice of South Australia: the playgrounds are about 5 acres in extent. There are several charities; of these the church lands produce £160 yearly for the relief of the poor inhabitants and for the repairing and maintaining church, church house and almshouses. The Fortescue charity, of the yearly value of £75, is for the free education of poor children. Miss Harrington's charity, amounting to £5 yearly, is for distribution to the poor; and several smaller sums are distributed on Good Friday. Paul Augustine Kingdon esq. of 29 Marlborough hill, St. John's Wood, London N.W. is lord of the manor.

Mr Clarke, the postman from Highampton, arriving outside Shebbear post office.

A cottage on the Shebbear Road, c. 1887.

Bridgman Samuel
Brownswood Frank M.Sc., F.C.S., F.I.C. (science master), The College
Clarke Albert Bleckly
Earle Mrs. Lovacott
Fox Rev. Thomas Edward (vicar)
Lark Rev. William Blake (governor), The College
Mackinley Samuel John M., B.A. (house master), The College
Ruddle Thomas B.A. (head master), Bible Christian college
Thorne Mrs. S. L. Holroyd house

COMMERCIAL.

Ackland Thos. shoe maker, New inn
Adams John, farmer, Worden
Adams John, yeoman, South Furse
Ayre Alfred, New inn P.H
Bale & Pett, job masters
Bale Henry, carpenter, Splot
Balkwill Catherine & Grace Damrel (Misses), grocers & drapers
Balsdon William, farmer, Wooda
Batten William, cowkeeper, New inn
Beer John, farmer, Berry
Bible Christian Connexional College (Rev. Wm. Blake Lark, governor; Thomas Ruddle B.A. head master; Samuel John M. Mackinley B.A. house master; Frank Brownswood M.Sc., F.C.S., F.I.C. science master)
Blight Richard, refreshment house
Bond John, farmer, Barn moor
Bridgman Amos, farmer, Vaddicott
Bridgman Arscott, farmer, Penicknold
Bridgman Frederick, farmer, Ruxhill
Broad Samuel, blacksmith & farmer, Badworthy moor
Brook James, carpenter & farmer, Caute hill
Cobbledick Richard, farmer, Furze

Chamberlain Grace (Mrs.), farmer, Ladford
Clarke Albert Bleckly L.R.C.S.Edin., L.S.A. surgeon & medical officer & public vaccinator, Shebbear district, Torrington union
Cobbledick Lewis, farmer & job-master, Forda
Corey Harriet (Mrs.), farmer, Hay
Crocker Isaac, cowkeeper
Curtis Wm. cowkeeper, Rigby's hay
Daniel William, farmer, Backway
Davey Henry, machinist, Barn park
Down John, blacksmith
Durant William, farmer, Moor
Elliott Herbt. Hayman, frmr. Libbear
Ellis Wm. & Sons, coach builders, cart, van & waggon builders, wheelwrights, blacksmiths, carpenters, joiners & builders &c. Folly cross
Fishleigh John, farmer, Moortown
Fry Thomas, school attendance officer
Gilbert John, farmer, Binworthy (letters through Torrington)
Gloin Edward, farmer, Smokey house
Griffin Arscott, farmer
Griffin Thomas, farmer, Allacott
Griffin Wm. Hy. farmer, Highfield
Heard John, farmer, Wootton moor
Heard Thos. farmer, Libbear Barton
Heard Wm. miller (water), Dipper mill
Hearn Henry, carpenter
Hill James, shoe maker
Hockin James, tailor &c
Hocking William, cowkeeper, Pauls
Hocking Wm. farmer, Cross Willis
Horn Arscott, hay & straw dealer
Hunkin Wm. Hy. frmr. Combe bridge
Kellaway George, shoe maker
Larkworthy William, farmer & butcher, Pitt villa

Larkworthy Mary (Mrs.), frmr.Berry
Leach William, jun. farmer & poultry dealer, Manna park
Ley Henry, farmer, Durpley (letters through Torrington)
Mill George, Devonport inn & farmr
Milman Samuel, farmer, Rowden
Milman William, farmer, Badworthy
Nethacott Ann (Mrs.), cowkeeper
Newcombe Thomas, farmer, Forda
Nichols Wm. Booth, frmr. Damping hl
Paige Harriet (Mrs.),shopkpr.New inn
Paige James, cowkeeper, New inn
Palmer Wm. Francis, registrar of births & deaths & vaccination officer for Shebbear sub-district
Palmer Richard, farmer, Post office
Pett John, farmer, Barn
Pett John Thorne, farmer, Paddon
Pett Samuel, farmer, Penicknold
Pope Wm. farmer, Little Ladford
Quance James, yeoman, Wooton
Quance Richard, farmer, Ruxhill
Reddaway Henry Richard, machinist
Slade James, stone & monumental mason, New inn
Spearman George, farmer, Ashe
Squance Richard, yeoman, Hay
Squance William Richard, farmer, Little South Hay
Squire Mary (Mrs.) & Sons, farmers, White
Squire Wm. jun. cowkpr. Ashbottom
Vanstone Stephen (exors. of), farmers & millers (water), Ladford mill
Vanstone Stephen Lewis, frmr. Caute
Walter William, farmer, Hill
Ward John, farmer, South Combe
White Elizabeth (Mrs.) (exors. of), farmers, Caute moor
White Jn. jun. frmr. Badworthy mr

104

SHEEPWASH (or Shipwash), formerly a considerable market town, is a small village and parish, 6 miles north-by-east from Halwill and Beaworthy station on the Okehampton and Holsworthy branch of the London and South Western railway, 5 north-west from Hatherleigh and 10 south from Torrington, in the Western division of the county, hundred of Shebbear, petty sessional division of Hatherleigh, union and county court district of Torrington, rural deanery of Torrington, archdeaconry of Barnstaple and diocese of Exeter. There is a bridge here, over the Torridge, of 5 arches, constructed at the expense of John Tosbury, who devised lands, now producing £50 yearly, for its maintenance. The church of St. Lawrence, rebuilt in 1880 at a cost of about £1,600, is an edifice of stone in the Early English style, consisting of vestry and organ chamber, nave, south porch and an embattled western tower with pinnacles, completed in 1889 at a cost of £300, with stone presented by Lord Clinton, and containing 6 bells, hung in the same year, at a cost of £360: each bell has an inscription taken from the 65th Psalm: the whole of the windows are stained, and the chancel retains two sedilia, and has a hammer beam roof, enriched with figures of angels holding trumpets: there is also within the church a fine modern screen at the west end, erected on the completion of the tower: the font is Norman: the interior has been reseated, and the new seats incorporate a quantity of old oak belonging to the church: there are now 103 sittings. The register of baptisms dates from the year 1673; burials and marriages, 1675. The living is a vicarage, net yearly value £112, in the gift of the Lord Chancellor, and held since 1892 by the Rev. Philip Alderton Highmore B.A. of Queen's College, Oxford. Here are Baptist and Bible Christian chapels. The Foresters' Hall is a substantial building of stone, erected in 1878, and will seat 250 people; the Court "Vale of Torrington, No. 4888," holds its meetings here. Upcott Avenel, formerly the seat of property and residence of John B. Coham-Fleming esq. D.L., J.P. Lord Clinton is lord of the manor and principal landowner. The soil is dun; subsoil, clay and stone. The chief crops are wheat, barley and oats. The area is 2,015 acres of land and 17 of water; rateable value, £1,763; the population in 1901 was 326.

Sexton, John Moast.

Post Office.—John Cutland Pedrick, sub-postmaster. Letters from Highhampton R.S.O. North Devon, received at 6.45 a.m.; dispatched at 5.50 p.m. Postal orders are issued here, but not paid. The nearest money order office is at Black Torrington & telegraph office at Shebbear, 4 miles distant

Voluntary Church School (mixed), established in 1814; the present school, built in 1873, will hold 106 children; average attendance, 58; Walter Hewitt, master; Miss Elizabeth Newcombe, mistress

The Square.

Children in the main street, c. 1906.

Coham-Fleming John Blyth D.L., J.P. Upcott avenel
Grills Thomas, Church house
Highmore Rev. Philip Alderton B.A. (vicar), The Vicarage
Jennings George Joseph, Oak house

COMMERCIAL.

Balkwell John, millwright
Bassett Susannah (Mrs.), milliner & shopkeeper
Brook Richard, butcher & farmer
Cudmore Elizabeth (Mrs.), shopkeeper
Dufty John, farmer, Court
Essery Eliza (Miss), shopkeeper

Finnamore Richard, Halfmoon P.H. Foresters' hall
Follond William, farmer, Beara farm
Harvey Wm. shoe ma. & news agent
Hobbs Frederick William, farmer, South Gortleigh
Hocking John, farmer, Wooda
Howe John, corn dealer
Jeffery Lewis, mason
Jeffery Robert, stone mason
Leach (Geo. miller (water), Upcot ml
Lock Charles, thatcher
Lock John, farmer & thatcher, Dabs park
Lock Mary Ann (Mrs.), dress maker

Millman John, farmer, South hill
Moore Josiah, farmer, Swadacott
Newcombe Thomas, wheelwright & farmer, Balls park
Page Wm. Eastcott, farmer, Blackmote
Parsons Wm. carpntr. to Lord Clinton
Pedrick John Cutland, blacksmith, Post office
Pike William, farmer, Westover
Pope Thomas, farmer, New court
Portbury Henry Mark, saddler
Quick William, farmer, Lukes
Smale John, shopkeeper
Squance James, farmer, Upcott Barton

Another street scene in Shebbear.

The Parish Church of St Lawrence, rebuilt in 1881.

East Street. The butcher is standing in the road.

Log sawing. Mr and Mrs Newcombe stand in the centre; the engine was owned by Mr Heddon.

SOUTH MOLTON is an ancient market town, municipal borough, parish, head of a petty sessional division, union and county court district, with a station one mile north of the town on the Devon and Somerset branch of the Great Western railway, and is at the junction of the roads from Bampton, Tiverton and Crediton to Barnstaple; 12 miles south-east from Barnstaple, 18 north-west from Tiverton, 20 north-west from Crediton, 27 north-north-west from the city of Exeter, 35 west from Taunton and 197 from London by railway, via Exeter, while the distance by road from London is only 182 miles; it is in the Northern division of the county, hundred and rural deanery of South Molton, archdeaconry of Barnstaple and diocese of Exeter.

The town is recorded as a borough as early as 1301; Queen Elizabeth granted it a charter in 1590, which was confirmed and enlarged by Charles II. whose charter remained in force until the passing of the Municipal Corporations Act, 1835 (5 and 6 William IV. c. 76), and the Corporation now consists of sixteen members, viz.:—a mayor, four aldermen and twelve common councilmen. The borough has a commission of the peace and separate court of quarter sessions, and petty sessions are held here for the South Molton division.

South Molton derives its name from the river Mole, on the western bank of which it is situated : this considerable stream is utilised to propel the machinery of the shirt and collar factory in the town, and of the great number of corn mills on its banks, connected here by a substantial bridge of one arch, built in place of one destroyed by a storm in October, 1841 ; the stream eventually falls into the river Taw, about 8 miles from the town. Broad street, East street, South street and West street are the principal thoroughfares. It is well lighted with gas, from works purchased by the Corporation in 1896, for £3,300, and was completely drained in 1868, and in 1869 the council of the borough established a water supply at a cost of £6,000, one half of the amount being given from North Molton parish, near Exmoor, 5 miles north of the town, and the water obtained is remarkably pure ; the filter beds were given by the late Alderman Smyth.

The Devon and Somerset branch of the Great Western railway, 42½ miles in length, from Taunton to Barnstaple, passes through the parish : a viaduct, nearly a quarter of a mile in length and 100 feet high, carries it over the river Bray in Castle Hill park. The Municipal Charity Trustees have improved and widened the road leading from the town to the station, a sum of £750 having been expended for that purpose.

East Street, South Molton. What a difference from today, with all the busy traffic going through the town.

Town Hall, South Molton.

The Guildhall.

The Congregational chapel was erected in 1834, on the site of the old church of 1700. There are 450 sittings.

The Wesleyan Methodist chapel, at the top of Duke street, erected in 1882-3 at a cost of £1,800, on the site of the old chapel built in 1821, is a building of stone, with dressings of Hambdon and Doulton stone, in the Florid Gothic style, and has sittings for 350 persons; in the rear of the chapel are schoolrooms.

The Baptist chapel is of stone, and affords sittings for 250 persons; the Mission hall, formerly a Primitive Methodist chapel, built in 1889, has 300 sittings; there is also a Bible Christian chapel, seating 180 persons, and a chapel for the Brethren, holding about 200 persons.

The Cemetery, in Mill street, opened in 1856, and since enlarged, covers an area of nearly four acres; there are two chapels, and a lodge for the keeper was built in 1882; it is under the control of a burial board of nine members.

The Guildhall is a building of Portland stone in the Italian style, and includes a turret containing a clock with three dials; the Council chamber is built on arches, projecting into the street.

The County Police Station in South street, is a fine building, with spacious offices, and quarters for sergeants and constables, and was erected in 1894 at a cost of about £2,500.

The Working Men's Reading Room, instituted by the daughters of the late Alderman Smyth, is governed by a committee of members and is supported by members' fees and voluntary contributions.

The Market-house was erected in 1863. The market days are Thursday and Saturday.

Cattle markets are held the first Thursday in every month. Fairs are held on the third Wednesday in June and the Wednesday after August 25th.

The early closing day is on Wednesday, at 3 p.m.

The Assembly Rooms, which occupy the upper storey of the New Market, are elegant and spacious, and will hold 400 persons; they are used for concerts, entertainments and public meetings, for which they are exceedingly well adapted.

There is a sawing mill near the Railway station; a shirt collar and blouse factory, a tannery and leather dressing establishment, in East street, coach building works, and the agricultural implement and engineering works of the Star Agricultural Engineering Co. Limited.

The South Molton Race Meeting, over the Kingsland course, is held on the Thursday after the old fair in August. The Kennels of the South Molton Subscription Harriers are situated here.

Barnstaple Street.

John Hill's shop, South Street.

T.H. Vicary's corn and seed warehouse, Barnstaple Street.

COMMERCIAL.

Adams Ann (Mrs.), greengrocer & florist, Catsease cottage
Adams Bessie (Miss), girls' school, Church street
Adams Mary Ann (Miss), dress maker, 42 South street
Adams Wm. Hobbs, collector of borough rates, Church st
Aggott Edward, shoe maker, 6 Barnstaple street
Amy Henry Cotton, house decorator, 52 South street
Ashelford Samuel, grocer, 9 Broad street
Askew Elizabeth (Miss), milliner, 2 East street
Askew Elizabeth (Mrs.), photographer, 8 East street
Assembly Rooms (Wm. Bulled, hall keeper), New market
Austin John, colporteur, 7 New road
Avery Charles, farmer, Brembridge
Ayre Sydney Herbert, agent for Norwich Union Fire Insurance Co. Gunsdown villas
Ayres Edmund, confectioner, 4 South street & shoe maker, 10 King street
Ayres Walter, boot & shoe maker, 28 Broad street
Babbage Edmund Tout, registrar of births & deaths & relieving & vaccination officer for the South Molton district, & school attendance officer, 1 Albany ter.North rd
Baker James, Unicorn hotel, Queen street
Baker Thomas, cattle dealer, 99 East street
Bale John Henry, grocer, 121 East street
Barrow William, farmer, Little Cockerham
Bater & Son, general ironmongers, 67 & 68 South street
Bawden Edith (Mrs.), Star temperance hotel, East street
Bawden Richard, manager to Star Agricultural Engineering Co. Limited, East street
Bawden William, saddler, 19 East street
Beer James, King's Arms P.H. & jobmaster, King street
Bendle John Huxtable, farmer, Meeth
Bennett Henry, whitesmith & range maker, 110 East street
Bennett William, rope, twine & bag maker, 13 Duke street
Bird George Westcott, ironmonger & smith & agricultural implement maker, 103a, East street
Bird Matthew James, seed, wool & manure merchant & emigration & insurance agent, 8 Duke street
Bird Thomas, dairyman, 130 East street
Blackford & Son, auctioneers, valuers, land agents & surveyors & insurance agents, 1 South street
Blackford John (firm, Blackford & Son), assessor & collector of taxes & sheriff's officer, 1 South street
D'ake John, veterinary surgeon & veterinary inspector to Board of Agriculture & County Council,14 & 15South st
Bowden & Co. biscuit bakers, 3 Cook's cross
Bowden Elizabeth (Mrs.), milliner, 17 South street
Bowden John, plumber & decorator, 14 Broad street
Bowden William, beer retailer & shopkpr. 1 Cook's cross
Braddick Albt.manager,Municipal Gas works,Parsonage la
Brayley George, sexton, Cemetery lodge
Brayley John, haulier, 5 Mill street
Brayley John, jun. road contractor, Cook's cross
Brearley Bernard H. mineral water manufr. 39 South st
Brewer & Son, coach builders, 102 & 103 East street
Bridgman Charles, Rose & Crown P.H. 8 South street & fellmonger, Cook's cross
Brown Sidney Stuckey, chemist & druggist & agent for W. & A. Gilbey Limited, wine & spirit merchants, & Royal Insurance, 33 Broad street
Buckingham John, farmer, North Aller
Bulled James, basket maker, 116 East street
Bulled Susan (Mrs.), grocer & china dealer, 133 East st

Bulled William, bailiff & town crier & school attendance officer & bill poster, Town hall
Burgess John, tailor, Stag's head
Burgess William Cole, hair dresser & tobacconist,4 Broad st
Barnett Elizabeth (Miss), boarding house, 1 Sunnyside
Bushen James, china & glass warehouse, 2a, Broad street
Cemetery (Frederic Day, clerk to burial board), Mill street
Chant Robert, wine & spirit merchant, 21 Broad street
Chapple Thomas, agent to the Devon & Exeter Savings Bank & borough treasurer, 2 South street
Church of England Temperance Society (Rev. Jas. Day, hon. sec.), Temperance hall, New road
Clarke Charles, watch maker & jeweller, 29 Broad street
Clarke William, farmer & baker, 2 Barnstaple street
Cobley Andrew William, draper, 27 East street
Cobley John, tinman & plumber, Duke street
Cock Robert & Sons, timber & coal merchants, Hacche sawing & grinding mills
Cock Robert, farmer & dairy, 12 South street
Cole Francis, wheelwright, South street
Cole Frederick John, farmer, Higher Blackpool
Cole Richard, tailor, 2 King street
Cole Samuel, farmer, Ford down
Cole Samuel, farmer, Higher Blackpool
Collacott Sarah (Mrs.), private school, 4 New road
Comins James, ironmonger, 75 South street
Cottage Hospital (Mrs. Dudley Bush, hon. sec.; Nurse S. Backhouse, matron), 69 South street
Cotty John, carpenter, Church street
County Court (His Honor Cecil Hugh W. Beresford B.A. judge; Frederic Day, registrar & high bailiff; Fredk. Bullen Wyatt, deputy registrar; Frank Moore, acting bailiff), Guildhall, Broad street
County Police Station (Capt. Walter Joseph Pelly, supt.), South street
Crocker George Henry, manager of Fox, Fowler & Co.'s Bank, 1 East street
Crosse, Day & Crosse, solicitors, 9 East street
Crosse Reginald Stawell, solicitor, perpetual commissioner & commissioner for oaths, 25 Broad street ; & at Chulmleigh & Witheridge
Crudge John, boot maker, 7 East street
Cruwys Edwin, wholesale pork dealer, 12 East street & livery stables, South street
Cruwys Mary (Mrs.), apartments, 1 West street
Dauncey Sarah Jane (Mrs.), dress maker, 2 New road
Davey Thomas, butcher, & Golden Lion P.H. 7 South st
Day Frederic F.R.G.S. (firm, Crosse, Day & Crosse), solicitor, perpetual commissioner & commissioner for oaths, clerk to county magistrates South Molton division, burial board, registrar & acting high bailiff of county court & clerk to the South Molton Rural District Council, East street
Dayment John Edward, blacksmith, North road
Delbridge John, umbrella maker, 7 King street
Dennis William, carrier, 37 East street
Densem Emma (Mrs.), farmer & dairy, Townhouse
Densem James Ernest, assistant overseer, collector of poor rates & agent for Northern Assurance Co. South street
Devon & Cornwall Banking Co. Limited (branch) (John Mortimore, manager), East street ; draw on Barclay & Co. Limited, London E C
Down John, decorator, 1 Alexandra terrace

112

Devon & Exeter Savings Bank (branch of) (Thos. Chapple, agent), 2 South street
Dockings Robert Hancock, agricultural implement maker, thrashing machine proprietor, blacksmith, machinist & wheelwright, Clappery Mill
Drake Elizabeth Ann (Miss), shopkeeper, 21 Barnstaple st
Eldridge Joseph Edwin, grocer & mineral water manufacturer, 6 Queen street
Elworthy Charles Morris, farmer, East Stone
Elworthy William, farmer, Honiton Barton
Facey Samuel, Hare & Hounds P.H. 38 East street
Farley Thomas, linen & woollen draper, 20 Broad street
Fewings John, poulterer, see Trick & Fewings
Fisher Mary Jane (Miss), dress maker, 13 South street
Flashman William, saddler, 24 Barnstaple street
Ford John, jobmaster, East street & Cook's cross
Foster Henry, inland revenue officer, Gunsdown villas
Fox, Fowler & Co. bankers (George Henry Crocker, manager), 1 East street ; draw on Barclay & Co. Limited, London E C
Frayne William, farmer, 2 West street
Freemasons' Hall (Loyal Lodge of Industry, No. 421; John Mortimore, hon. sec. ; Fortescue Lodge of Mark Master Masons, No. 9; Attree Powell,hon. sec.),New rd
Gas Works (Municipal) (Russell Louis Riccard, sec. ; Albert Braddick, manager), Parsonage lane
Gaydon George, farmer, West Clatworthy
Gebbett James Albert Kingdon, saddler, 105 East street
George Private, Family & Commercial Hotel (S. P. Kelland, proprietor), ladies' & gentlemen's hacks & hunters always on hire, good stabling, loose boxes or lock-up coach houses; posting in all its branches; good trout-fishing free, Broad street
Gordon Amelia (Miss), preparatory school, 25 South street
Guildhall (William Bulled, hall keeper), Broad street
Hall Frederick John, assistant supt. Prudential Assurance Co. 4 Albany terrace
Hammett Alfred James, saddler, 9 King street
Hammett Mary Ann (Mrs.), dress maker, 9 King street
Hammond Fredk Saml. watch ma. & jeweller, 5 East st
Hancock John, farmer, Middle Blackpool
Harris Charles Frederick, Tiverton inn, 20 East street
Harris Joseph Bastable, chemist & wine & spirit merchant, 18 Broad street
Harvey Hamilton James, draper, 17 Broad street
Haskings Benjamin, carrier, Mill street
Hawkes William Henry, mace bearer to the coroporation, 4 Alfred place
Hearn Charles, farrier, 13 West street
Herbert Edward, collegiate school
Hill Ernest, Anchor inn, 66 South street
Hill Jessie (Mrs.), Tinto hotel, Station road
Hill John, draper, hatter & hosier, 72, 73 & 74 South street
Hill John, farmer, South Aller
Hodge George, baker. 129 East street
Hodge John Samuel, linen & woollen draper, tailor, hatter, hosier & outfitter, 24 & 25 Broad street
Holcombe Nathaniel John, builder, 23 East street
Holman James, baker, 49 West street
Holmes Heber, saddler & harness maker ; bags, portmanteaus &c. 2 Broad street
Howe William Nott, tailor & habit maker, 8 East street
Huxtable Chas. Geo. Pearce, egg & poultry dlr. 1 King st
Huxtable George Henry, postmaster, Post office, Broad st
Huxtable John Chas. tailor & poultry breeder, 54 South st
Jutsum Richard, relieving & vaccination officer & registrar of births & deaths for Witheridge sub-district & collector to guardians & school attendance officer, South Molton union, 18 South street
Kelland Robert, surveyor & sanitary inspector to the Rural District Council, George hotel, Broad street
Kelland Sylvanus P. George private, family & commercial hotel ; posting in all its branches ; good fishing free, Broad street
Kemp John Amos, butcher, 22 East street
Kendle Frederic Wellesley, surgeon, Hawthornden
Kingdon Emily H. (Miss), baker, 53 South street
Kingdon Hargreaves, grocer & provision merchant, 26 Broad street & 27 East street
Kingdon Henry, hair dresser, fancy repository & tobacconist, 124 East street
Kingdon Henry, ironmonger, 131 East street
Kingdon John, fellmonger & wool dealer, 53 South street
Kingdon John Keys, cabinet maker, 11 Duke street
Kingdon Joseph, accountant, sec. to South Molton United schools, to South Molton & Barnstaple Annuitant Society & to South Molton & North Devon Provident Society, 46 West street
Kingdon Lucy (Miss), milliner, 82 East street
Kingdon William, master of workhouse, North road
Knill William, boot & shoe maker, 70 South street
Lethbridge Elizabeth (Mrs.), grocer, 10 South street

Lethbridge William, marine store dealer, 11 Mill street
Lewis Lionel, cabinet ma. & furniture dlr. 6 South st
Leyman Richard, sergeant of police, South street
Lock John, shoe maker, 88 East street
Loyal Fortescue Lodge (5,898) I.O.O.F.M.U. (W. H. Fuke, sec.), Town Arms hotel, East street
Lyddon Eleanor (Miss), teacher of music, 96 & 97 East st
Lyddon John, musical instrument warehouse & pianoforte tuner, 96 & 97 East street
Madge William Acland, deputy registrar of marriages, 13 Barnstaple street
Manning Elizabeth (Mrs.), farmer, Neelstwood
Manning Susannah (Mrs.), apartments, 17 East street
Martin Arthur Walter Cross, ironmonger, 23 Broad street
Martin John, fishmonger & refreshment rooms, 8 King st
Mason Mary Ann (Mrs.), laundress, 9 Barnstaple street
Mears Frederick, foreman to Mr.Charles Morris Elworthy, Combrew
Merson Frank, dental surgeon, 36 East street
Moor & Son, coach builders & harness factors, 56 & 58 South street
Moore John, farm bailiff to Mr. Wm. Hulland, Furze Bray
Moore John, Ring of Bells, Duke street
Mortimore John, manager of the Devon & Cornwall Bank, East street
Mothersdale John, manager of the National Provincial Bank & treasurer to the union & Rural District Council, Broad street
Mothersdale John, insurance agent for Liverpool, London & Globe Fire Insurance Co., Accident Insurance Co. Limited & Clerical, Medical & General Life Assurance Co. Broad street
Mountjoy George Huxtable, draper, tailor & outfitter, 31 Broad street & 136 East street
Mountjoy William, woolstapler &c. see Sanders & Mountjoy
National Provincial Bank of England Limited (branch) (John Mothersdale, manager), Broad street ; draw on head office, 112 Bishopsgate within, London E C
Norman John, dairyman, Hill
Northam John, dairyman, 32 West street
Norton Charles, grocer, 46 South street
Nott John, farmer, Cockerham
Nott Samuel, game dealer, West street
Nunn Emily (Miss), dress maker, 31 West street
Nutt Elizabeth G. (Miss), dress maker, 12 Duke street
Paige John Gillard, chemist & druggist, 76 South street
Palfreyman Wm. mace bearer to the corporation,South st
Parker William, butcher, 16 South street
Passmore Mary & Bertha (Misses), ladies' schl. 18 East st
Patey Mary (Mrs.), dairy, Churchyard
Pearce Charles, tanner, currier, leather merchant & leather dresser (black & brown harness), East street
Phillips Amanda Hannah (Mrs.), temperance hotel & fancy repository, 28 East street
Phillips John, cabinet maker, 28 East street
Pinn William, shopkeeper, 3 Barnstaple street
Pomeroy William Henry, jobmaster ; posting in all its branches ; lock-up coach house & loose boxes ; private apartments for families & commercials, 3 Broad street
Poole George, printer, stationer, bookbinder, bookseller, fancy goods repository, berlin wools,Broad st. & King st
Powell Attree, deputy supt. registrar, 2 East street & sub-distributor of stamps, Churchyard
Public Lending Library (Mrs. Annie Bulled, librarian), East street
Rawle John, farmer, Great Hele
Reed John, farmer, East Clatworthy
Riccard & Son, solicitors, & agents to the Commercial Union Assurance Co. Limited, Church yard
Riccard Russell Louis (firm, Riccard & Son), solicitor, town clerk, clerk of the peace & to the income tax commissioners, sec. to the Gas Works, & clerk to the guardians & assessment & school attendance committees of South Molton union, & supt. registrar of South Molton district, Church yard
Richards Ann (Miss), tea agent, Tout's court, East street
Rivers Walter, clothier & outfitter, 5 Broad street
Rowcliffe George John, butcher, 27 Barnstaple street
Royal North Devon Yeomanry Cavalry (Hussars) (C or South Molton squadron); Capt. M. De Las Casas, squadron commander; Capt. R. A. Sanders, 2nd in command ; Squadron-Sergt.-Major drill instructor
Rumbelow Mary Augusta (Miss), New inn, South street
Rumbelow Samuel, coal dealer &c. Cook's cross
Sanders & Mountjoy, woolstaplers, coal, lime, salt & building material merchants, South street & Station yard
Sanders & Smyth, surgeons, 112 Eas. street
Sanders W. & Son, builders, contractors & coal merchants, 119 East street & Station yard
Saunders William, poulterer, 36 South street

An earlier view of Barnstaple Street.

Sanders Edmund Augustin, miller, corn merchant & butcher, 98 East street; & at Lower Mole mills
Sanders Thomas F.R.C.S.Eng. (firm, Sanders & Smyth), surgeon, county coroner for South Molton district & medical officer & public vaccinator, Nos. 1, 4 & 10 districts, South Molton union, & med. officer of the workhouse, 112 East street
Searle George, blacksmith & tool maker, South street
Searle George, farmer & thatcher, Shallowford
Shapland J. T. & Son, solicitors, North street
Shapland Albert Edward (firm, Shapland J. T. & Son), solicitor, perpetual commissioner, commissioner for affidavits in the High Court & commissioner for taking affidavits in the court of the vice-warden of the Stannaries of Cornwall & Devon; offices, North street
Sims Joseph, draper & milliner, 7 & 8 Broad street
Skinner Alexander, farmer, West Ford
Skinner John, farmer, South hill
Skinner Francis, baker, 65 South street
Slader Charles, farmer & poultry breeder, Hacche Barton
Smith James, dairyman, 113 East street
Smith John, butcher, 108 East street
Smith John, registrar of marriages for South Molton union, 49 South street
Smyth Henry James L.R.C.P.Lond., M.R.C.S.Eng. (firm, Sanders & Smyth), surgeon, & medical officer & public vaccinator, 11th district, South Molton union, & medical officer Rechabites, 112 East street
South Molton Agricultural Association (John Blackford, sec.), 1 South street
South Molton Art School (Frederick William Gard, head master), North street
South Molton District Committee for Technical Education (Attree Powell, sec.), 2 East street
South Molton Constitutional Club (William Nott Horne, sec.), 2 South street
South Molton Fat Stock Society (John Blackford, hon. sec.), 1 South street
South Molton Gazette (A. R. Tucker & Son, publishers; Gregory & Son, proprietors), 12 Broad street
South Molton Liberal Association (James Sanders, president & hon. treasurer; J. S. Hodge, hon. sec.)
South Molton Races & Steeple Chases (A. E. Shapland, hon. sec. & treas.), North street
South Molton Shirt & Collar Manufacturing Co. Limited (Richard Shaymaker, manager)
South Molton Subscription Pack of Harriers (Messrs. S. P. Kelland & G. H. Crocker, joint masters)
South Molton United Schools (John Frederick Thrower, master; Joseph Kingdon, sec. & treas.), North street
Southcombe John, dairyman, Whitehall
Squire Alfred, Red Lion P.H. & butcher, Barnstaple street
Stanbury Richard, farmer, Coombe farm
Star Agricultural Engineering Co. Limited (The), agricultural implement manufacturers, engineers, tool makers, smith &c. (R. Bawden, manager; T. Snell, sec)
Stediford William, draper & milliner, 125 East street
Stoneman Thomas, farmer, South Ford
Symons Jane (Mrs.), dairy, Church street
Tall & Son, bakers &c. 126 & 127 East street
Tanner Lyddon, grocer, wine & spirit merchant & agent to the Commercial Union Assurance Co. 30 Broad street
Tapp John, boot maker, 14 West street
Taylor Jn. fish dlr. & common lodging-house, Gunswell ln
Temperance Hall (Mrs. Ann Berry, caretaker), New road
Thomas Alfred Jesse, farmer, Rock farm

Thomas William, builder, 10 Duke street
Thorne John, mason, 19 North street
Trawin John, ironmonger & wire worker, 118 East street
Trawin William Fredk. joiner & shopkeeper, 44 East st
Trick & Fewings, poulterers, 10 & 11 Broad street
Tucker A. R. & Son, printers & stationers, & publishing office of the "South Molton Gazette," 12 Broad street
Tucker & Son, chimney sweepers, 12 Mill street
Tucker Edward Collard, shipping agent, 12 Broad street
Tucker Lily C. (Miss), dress maker, 32 South street
Vernon John, butcher, 13 Broad street
Vicary Thomas Henry, corn, seed & manure merchant, 14 Barnstaple street
Vickery William, Barnstaple inn, 12 Barnstaple street
Volunteer Battalion (4th) Devonshire Regiment (G Co. Capt. W. H. Spehr; Philip Welch, sergt.-instructor), Armoury, East street
Walford Albert, wine merchant, 3 & 4 King street
Warren William, haulier, Cook's cross
Watson Charles Michael, professor of music & organist of St. Mary Magdalene's church, 19 Barnstaple street
Webb & Sons, manure & seed merchants (M. J. Bird, agent), Stores, Station road
Webb William James, accountant, clerk to the land tax commissioners for South Molton division, to the South Molton municipal charity trustees, & clerk & school attendance officer to the Romansleigh & Mariansleigh united district school board, & agent for the Law Life Assurance Society, Cook's cross
Webber Frederick, farmer, Snurridge
Webber John Galliford, watch maker, 25 East street
Webber Richard, farmer, Kingsland
Webber Richard, Town Arms P.H. 12 East street
Welch Philip, sergt.-instructor G. Co. 4th V.B. Devonshire Regiment, The Armoury, East street
Western Samuel, Red Cow P.H. & carpenter, 3 East street
White Thomas, insurance agent, 8 Oakland place, South st
Walgery Elizth. (Miss), dress & stay ma. 5 Barnstaple st
Walgery Samuel, cabinet maker & upholsterer, 22 Broad st
Wigham William Harper M.B.Durh., M.R.C.S.Eng. physician, & medical officer of health for the borough, certifying factory surgeon & medical officer & public vaccinator No. 9 district, South Molton union & No. 11 district, Barnstaple union, Moleford house
Williams William & Son, coal, corn &c. dealers & poulterers, 50 West street
Williams Chas. grocer, & brewer's agent, 19 Broad street
Williams William, shoe maker, 100 East street
Wills Thomas, cycle maker, 10 Barnstaple street
Wood Henry John, colt breaker & horse trainer, & dairyman, Mill street
Wootton Allen Shakespeare, borough surveyor, sanitary inspector & waterworks engineer, Town hall
Working Men's Reading Room (Wm. H. Fuke, hon. sec. & treas.), Broad street
Wright William Charles, horse trainer, Cook's cross
Wyatt Frederick Bullen, solicitor, clerk to the borough magistrates & deputy registrar of County Court, 9 East street
Yeandle Laura (Miss), confectioner, 29 Barnstaple street
Yendell Fred, farmer, Lordsdown
Young Men's Christian Association (Daniel Richards, hon. sec.), East street
Young Women's Christian Association (Miss Dighton, hon sec.), 9 Barnstaple street

114

ST. GILES-IN-THE-WOOD is a parish and village, 3 miles east from Torrington station on the London and South Western railway, in the Northern division of the county, Fremington hundred, Torrington petty sessional division, union and county court district, and in the rural deanery of Torrington, archdeaconry of Barnstaple and diocese of Exeter. The church of St. Giles is an edifice of stone, consisting of chancel, nave of five bays, aisles, transepts and an embattled western tower with pinnacles, containing a clock and 6 bells; the former tenor bell was given in 1697 by Sir John Rolle K.B. of Stevenstone, and was re-cast at the expense of John, 2nd and last Baron Rolle, in 1823, when the peal of 5 was re-cast into 6, by Messrs. W. and J. Taylor, of Oxford; weight of tenor is 10 cwt.; at the west end is a recumbent effigy and brass, dated 1648, to Thomas Chafe esq. of Doddiscott, brother-in-law of Tristram Risdon, the historian; in the church is also a brass effigy with inscription to Alyanora (Cople-ston), wife of John Pollard, ob. 1430; another brass, with effigies of a lady and 10 children, and an inscription to Margaret (Forde) wife of John Rolle, of Stevenstone, ob. 1592; at the foot of the brass are the arms of Forde; a third, with effigy of a lady and inscription to Joan (Pollard), wife of William Risdon, of Winscott, gent. ob. 1610; and one other to John Rolle above-named, ob. 1570: the reredos and pulpit are of alabaster, with carved marble columns; and there are several stained windows; the church was restored in 1863 at a cost of £2,000, by the Hon. Mark George Kerr Rolle, who also in part defrayed the expense of further alterations made in 1879, when an organ chamber and vestry were built, a new clock placed in the tower and the bells restored: the church affords about 500 sittings. The register dates from the year 1556. The living is a vicarage, net yearly value £41, with residence and 2½ acres of glebe, in the gift of the Hon. Mark G. K. Rolle, and held since 1878 by the Rev. Harry John Wilmot-Buxton M.A. of Brase-nose College, Oxford. The great tithe is appropriated to Christ Church, Oxford. There is a Wesleyan chapel, and a service room for Baptists. A reading room and library, containing 300 volumes, was opened in 1867, and is sup-ported by subscriptions. There are four almshouses for aged women, with an endowment of £5 yearly, and charities of £8 yearly value, besides several other charities. Way was formerly the residence of the Way family: it is now the property of the trustees of the late Ven. Charles Wellington Furse M.A., J.P. archdeacon and canon resi-dentiary of Westminster (d. 1900). Stevenstone, the family mansion of the Rolle family, standing in a deer park of 300 acres, was rebuilt of stone in 1872, and is the seat of the Hon. Mark George Kerr Rolle D.L., J.P. who is lord of the manor, and with H. F. Furse esq. is chief landowner. The soil is sandy; subsoil, stone. The chief crops are cereal. The area is 4,990 acres of land and 24 of water; rateable value, £3,349; the population in 1901 was 623.

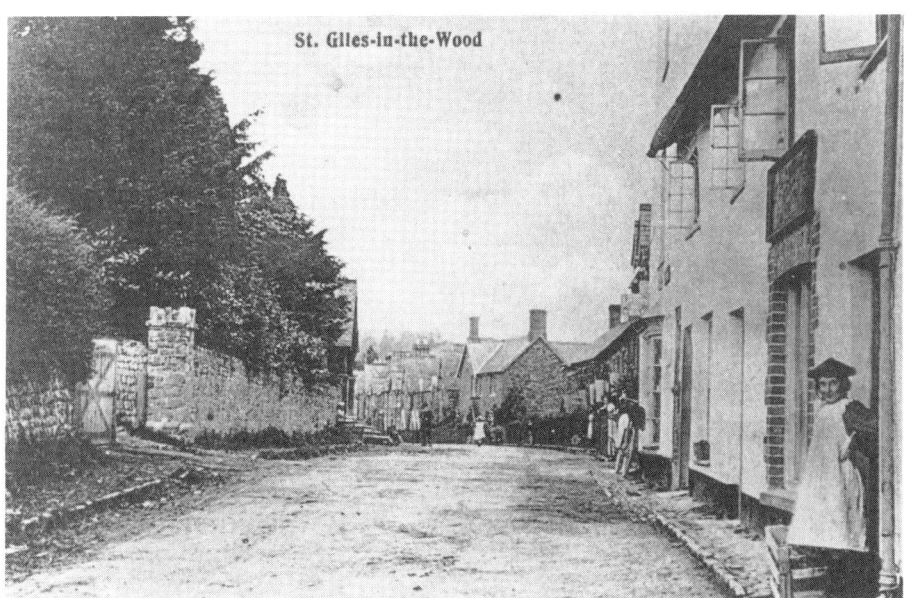

St. Giles-in-the-Wood

St Giles-in-the-Wood village street, c. 1902. Winnie Luxton is standing outside Samuel Luxton's grocery shop. The postman's bicycle is leaning against the bow-window of Mrs Trick's post office.

Stevenstone House.

DODSCOTT is a hamlet 1 mile north-east. The family of Clarke resided here for many generations; but the place is now owned by the Hon. Mark Rolle. WINSCOTT, 1 south-east formerly belonged to the Risdons, and was subsequently sold by the Northcotes to the Hon. Mark Rolle; KINGSCOTT, three-quarters of a mile south; HIGH BULLEN, 1 north; HEALAND, 1½ south-west are also hamlets.

Sexton, William Clemens.

Post Office.—Walter Trick, sub-postmaster. Letters through Torrington, arrive at 8.30 a.m.; dispatched at 5.40 p.m. week days only. Postal orders are issued here, but not paid. Torrington, 3 miles distant, is the nearest money order & telegraph office

Wall Letter Box, Kingscott, cleared at 5.25 p.m. week days only

Public Elementary School (mixed), built in 1860, for 230 children; average atendance, 126; & supported in part by the Hon. Mark G. Kerr Rolle; William Knott, master; Miss B. A. Knott & Miss E. J. Derrick,assistnts

ST. GILES-IN-THE-WOOD.

Burnett Capt. William Gordon
Johnson Miss, Rose moor
Rolle Hon. Mark George Kerr D.L., J.P. Stevenstone; & Carlton club, London S W
Wilmot-Buxton Rev. Harry John M.A. Vicarage

COMMERCIAL.

Balman Edmund, farmer, Ward
Barrie James, forester
Bowman John, farmer, Great Huish
Brown Samuel,farm bailiff to the Hon. M. G. K. Rolle, Peagham
Copp Henry, farmer, Cranford
Folland Thomas, farmer, Beara
Gillies William, head gardener to Hon. M. G. Kerr Rolle, Stevenstone

Haggett Thomas, head gamekeeper
Hammett John, farmer, Higher & Lower hill
Hookway John, farmer & butcher, Town tenement
Hookway William, farmer, Way
Hookway Wm. H. farmer, Stoney ford
Knott Wm. organist & music teacher
Luxton Samuel, shopkeeper & farmer
Millman John, farmer, Winscott
Page John William, farmer, Whittisleigh Barton
Passmore Henry, clerk of works
St. Giles' Reading Room & Library (William Knott, sec)
Squire Thomas, farmer, Ley
Tanton Thomas, farmer, Ley
Trick Walter, farmer & shopkeeper, Post office

DODSCOTT.

Guard Richard, farmer, East Dodscott
Lemon Thomas, boot maker
Squire William Henry, farmer

KINGSCOTT.

Friend Thomas, jun. shopkeeper
Hookway Charles, farmer, Higher ho
Hookway William Brinsmead (Mrs.), farmer & butcher, Flavils

HIGH BULLEN.

Clemens Thomas, blacksmith & farmer
Couch Frederick, boot & shoe maker

HEALAND.

Cole Samuel, farmer, North Healand
Jewell Grace(Mrs.),frmr. Sth.Healand

Private Thomas Clemens, North Devon Yeomanry, son of Thomas Clemens, blacksmith, c. 1880s.

Cyril Folland, Ley Farm.

A group of children in the main street. The boy in the foreground is Keith Giles, Joan Clarke is on the steps. From left to right: Thomas Finnimore, Jim Clarke, Nellie Finnimore, Edna Clarke, -?-, -?- and Hilda Clarke.

SUTCOMBE is a parish and village 6 miles north from Holsworthy station, on a branch of the London and South Western railway, in the Western division of the county, Black Torrington hundred, Holsworthy petty sessional division, union and county court district, rural deanery of Holsworthy, archdeaconry of Barnstaple and diocese of Exeter: the river Waldon flows through the parish and is crossed by a stone bridge of one arch. The church of St. Andrew is a very ancient building of stone, in the Norman and later styles, consisting of chancel, nave, north and south chapels, north aisle and a small western tower, There is no manor. The principal landowners are the trustees of the late W. Yeo esq. The soil is light loam; subsoil, clay and stone rubble. The chief crops are oats and wheat. The area is 2,872 acres of land and 6 of water; rateable value, £1,441; the population in 1901 was 281.

By Local Government Board Order, 14,690, a detached part of this parish known as Little Sutcombe was transferred to Pancrasweek, March 24, 1884.

Sexton, Samuel Gerry.

Post Office.—Richard Hockin, sub-postmaster. Letters

Moving the motor after the accident at Sutcombe on 18 August 1909.

Banbury Mrs. Millbrook cottage
Braund Rev. Thomas (Bible Christian), Thuborough
Greig Octavius, Thuborough house
Ravenhill Rev. Wm. Henry, Rectory

COMMERCIAL.

Allin Daniel, farmer & miller (water) & sawing mill
Allin Norman, farmer, Thuborough Barton
Allin Wm. farmer & landowner, Town
Ayre Wm. blacksmith, Sutcombe mill
Baker James Hy. farmer, Hawkwill
Bartlett Bryant, farmer & landowner, New house

Bartlett Thomas, farmer, New house
Britton Charles, farmer, Langadon
Carter Joseph, farmer, Matcott
Cawsey John, farmer, Upcott
Cawsey Samuel Thomas, farmer, South lane & West Brendon
Cole Thomas, farmer, East Brendon
Daniel Frederick, farmer, Upcott
Davey Thomas, shoe maker & apartments
Fishleigh Robert, farmer, landowner & cattle dealer, East Paddon
Fry John, farmer & miller (water), Thuborough mill
Furse Charles Henry, farmer, Billhole
Gerry Samuel, shopkeeper

Gilbert Thomas, shopkeeper
Ham Albt. blacksmith, Sutcombe mill
Hockin Richard, tailor, Post office
Hodge Richard, shopkeeper
Jenkins Thos. frmr. North Lane farm
Jones John, farmer, Highborough
Jones William, carpenter
Jones William Hy. boot & shoe dealer
Millman Thos. farmer, West Paddon
Mountjoy Edmund, farmer & landowner, Sutcombe Mill farm
Parsons Samuel, builder, Hollands
Stacey Frederick, farmer, Lutson
Walter Rt. farmer & landowner, Heldon
Wickett Brothers, farmers, Northcot

MOTOR 'BUS ACCIDENT.

——:◇:——

POLICE-SERGEANT KILLED AT SUTCOMBE.

A distressing accident occurred at Sutcombe, near Holsworthy, on Wednesday evening. The Holsworthy Motor 'Bus " Devonia " was returning to Bradworthy from Holsworthy Market, full of passengers. While ascending Sutcombe Hill something went wrong with its mechanism. The 'bus commenced to run backwards, and Police-Sergt. Parnell, who was one of the inside passengers, attempted to get out. Just as his feet were touching the ground, however, the vehicle swerved to the right, and, upsetting, pulled the Sergeant under, with the result that he was killed on the spot.

The other 16 passengers were practically unhurt. Dr. Betts, of Bradworthy, was soon in attendance, as were also Drs. Kingdon and Gray, of Holsworthy. On examining the body of deceased, they found the back of the head completely crushed.

A newspaper report on the accident at Sutcombe, 18 August 1909.

TORRINGTON (GREAT) is a municipal borough, head of a union, county court district and petty sessional division, market town and parish, on the Torridge, here crossed by three bridges, at points respectively south-east, south-west and north-west of the town, and is at the junction of the roads from Barnstaple and South Molton to Tavistock and Plymouth; it is the terminus of a branch of the London and South Western railway, opened in 1872, 7 miles south-south-east from Bideford, 10 south-by-west from Barnstaple, 13 north from Okehampton and 225 from London, and is in the Northern division of the county, Fremington hundred, rural deanery of Torrington, archdeaconry of Barnstaple and diocese of Exeter. The town is beautifully situated on the top of a hill 300 feet high, from which an extensive view is obtained, overlooking the Torridge; is lighted with gas from works in Gas lane, and supplied with water from a reservoir at Blackerton, 2 miles from the town; waterworks were built in 1871, and in 1901 were considerably enlarged by the Corporation. A canal, nearly 5 miles long, was constructed by the late Lord Rolle, in 1823, from the town to the navigable part of the Torridge below Wear Gifford; at Beam there is a lofty stone aqueduct of 5 arches, but portions having been filled in it is not now in use. A part of this canal, between the station and the town mills, was about 1893 converted into a road. The road to Little Torrington was made by Lord Rolle in 1842. The borough sent members to Parliament in the reigns of Ed. I., II. and III. but was relieved of that burden at its own request. Torrington was incorporated by three charters, granted by Mary, James I. and James II. of which copies only now exist: the Corporation, under the provisions of the Municipal Corporations Act, 1835, consists of a mayor, four aldermen and eleven councillors. The borough has a commission of the peace, granted July 7th, 1893. The church of St. Michael is an edifice of stone in the Decorated style,

Fore Street decorated, possibly in 1911 for the Coronation of George V.

Torrington High Street.

In High street stands a drinking fountain of stone and granite, presented to the town by the Hon. Mark G. K. Rolle in August, 1870; it is 18 feet high and approached by two rows of steps, and in the upper portion is a clock. There are three banks, a Mutual Improvement Society, and a Conservative Working Men's Association, with a reading room and a library of about 600 volumes, in South street, and a Free Institute, in Halsdon terrace, opened in 1891, with a library of 700 volumes and reading and billiard rooms. The North Devon Freehold Land Society has its offices here. The Market House for meat, vegetables and poultry, erected by the Town Council in 1842, is a spacious building, and includes a large hall, let for lectures and exhibitions; in 1892 the central roof was covered in with glass, the expense being chiefly defrayed by the Hon. Mark G. K. Rolle. The market is held on Saturday and a sale of cattle, conducted by Henry Slee and Sons and Mr. G. D. Copp, is held on the last Saturday in every month; the market, which belongs to the Corporation, was in 1893 transferred to the New Public Cattle Market, erected in School lane, at a cost of £1,000. Annual fairs are held in the town on the third Saturday in March (Great Fair) and the first Thursday in May; on this day the Premium cattle show is held, and the second Thursday and two following days in October. Fairs were held here as early as 1226, but all the borough records were destroyed by fire in 1724. The manufacture of silk gloves is largely carried on, about 500 persons being employed in factories and in their own houses; the chief factory is that of Mr. William Vaughan, which is spacious and well-ventilated. Messrs. John Jackson and Mrs. Rudd also have glove factories here. There is also a large leather dressing establishment, carried on by Messrs. N. G. & M. Chapple, and the Torridge Vale butter factory of Messrs. R. Sandford and Son. The Fire Brigade, consisting of 30 men and one superintendent, has three manual engines, and is otherwise efficiently equipped. At Torrington is stationed the A squadron of the Royal North Devon Yeomanry Cavalry (Imperial Yeomanry) and the F Co. of the 4th Volunteer Battalion, Devonshire Regiment; the drill hall and armoury is in Calf street. The kennels of the Stevenstone fox hounds are at Rotherham Bridge, near here. There are almshouses for 22 poor persons, 6 being in the gift of the Hon. Mark G. K. Rolle, and the remaining 16 with the trustees of the Town and Alms Land Charities.

Mill Street, c. 1905.

Maypole dancing in the Square. A modern photograph of an ancient custom, fairs were held here as early as 1226.

An aerial view of Torrington, showing the medieval strip fields that were visibly still in use in the 1950s.

The Cottage Hospital was opened in October, 1897; the number of patients admitted in 1900 was 33, making a total of 84 since the Hospital was opened.

At the west end of the town is an extensive tract of common land, which has been laid out with walks made and furnished with seats as a public recreation ground, and part has been reserved for various kinds of outdoor sports; the whole is vested in a body of conservators under the "Great Torrington Commons Act, 1889."

In the sixth year of Richard I.'s reign the common land was given for the benefit of the poor by William FitzRobert, baron of Torrington.

Of Torridge Castle, erected by Richard de Merton in 1340, only a portion of the chapel, taken down in 1780 and now converted into a school, remains, and that part of Castle hill is now called "Barley Grove." Near the spot where the castle formerly stood is a column, erected in 1816 to commemorate the battle of Waterloo, fought June 18th, 1815. In 1484 the sessions were held at Torrington, at which the Marquis of Dorset, Sir Edward Courtenay, Bishop Peter Courtenay and about 500 others, were indicted for treason against Richard III. and outlawed, and Sir Thomas St. Ledger, who had married the king's sister, and Thomas Rayme esq. being found guilty of high treason, were beheaded at Exeter. The Lady Margaret Countess of Richmond and mother of Henry VII. resided much at Torrington in the old manor house, which she afterwards gave as a residence for the clergyman of the parish, whose parsonage was formerly at Priestacott; in 1590 the sessions were held here in consequence of the prevalence of the plague at Exeter, and Torrington, probably in consequence, also suffered from the same infection the following year. In 1643 the Parliamentary forces, advancing on this place from Bideford, were totally defeated by Colonel Digby. In February, 1646, Lord Hopton, having stationed his army at Torrington, which he fortified and barricaded, was attacked by Sir Thomas Fairfax, advancing from Chulmleigh by way of Stevenstone, on the night of the 16th, and after a severe action the royalists were completely worsted and eight colours taken, besides numerous prisoners, 200 of whom, being confined in the church, were destroyed, together with the guard, by the blowing up of nearly 80 barrels of powder, which had been deposited there by Lord Hopton, and very little of the church beyond the vestry escaped the effects of the explosion. In 1665 Tristram Arscott esq. gave the hospital of St. Mary Magdalen, founded at Taddiport by Lady Anne Butler, to Great Torrington and to the churchwardens of Little Torrington.

New Street around the turn of the century.

Flower pickers by Torrington church.

The commons and the railway station.

Mill Street.

NOTICE.

A Meeting of the Parties entitled to Commonable or other Rights over or in Great Torrington Common,

Situate in the Parish of Great Torrington, in the County of Devon, will be held

AT THE TOWN HALL, GREAT TORRINGTON, AFORESAID,

On Tuesday, the 14th day of October inst.,

At Seven o'Clock in the evening,

For the purpose of receiving an application from the Promoters of a Light Railway, for leave to carry their proposed Line through a portion of the said Common adjoining or near the Torrington Railway Station, and appointing a Committee to treat with such Promoters for the compensation to be paid for the same.

Dated this Sixth day of October, 1879.

Signed on behalf of the Promoters,

GEO. DOE,

Solicitor, Great Torrington.

A notice to Torrington Commoners, 1879.

Torrington Commoners guarding their rights.

Livingstone John James, 3 Queen's terrace, New street
Macartney Lieut.-Col. Arthur Sutherland, Salterns, South street
Macindoe James Gray, New street
Mallet Henry Leverton J.P. Blenheim
Martin Miss, New street
Medland William Cock, Windy cross
Morris Major-Gen. Robert, Beam
Morse Edward, South street
Owen Rev. George Frankling (Baptist), New street
Pollock Rev. Henry D. F., B.A. (curate), Calf street
Pye Rev. J. C. (Bible Christian), South street

Pope Henry, 217 New street
Rew Wm. P. Fair view, Mill street
Rude Percy J. 4 New street
Sandford George, 221 New street
Sandford Robert, Rolle road
Sheppard William George, Well street
Sillifant John Henry, 5 White's lane
Slee Frederick William, 20 Castle st
Slee Henry, The Warren
Smale Wm. Kempton cot. New street
Snow Reginald Maurice, 24 South st
Squire Henry, 200 New street
Squire Mrs. New street
Stawell George, Mill street
Steevenson Mrs. Rbt. Hy. Rockmnt
Sutcliff Edward Harvey M.B. Park vil

Sutcliff Mrs. Morton villa
Tucker Wm. South view, New street
Vaughan Miss C. 77 New street
Vaughan William J.P. South street
Vaughan Wm. Ford, West ho. New st
Weare Rev. William J. (Wesleyan Methodist), Wesley manse
Webber Silvanus, High street
Weeks Francis, 196 New street
Werry Arthur, 223 New street
Westland Mrs. Halsdon terrace
Wilkins Rev. Edward (Congregational), Howe manse, Castle street
Wills Miss, New street
Yonge Col. Charles W. Mill street
Yonge Miss, Mill street

COMMERCIAL.

Adams Brothers, tanners & curriers, South street
Alford John, farmer, Allen's Weeks
Allin Thomas, glove manufacturer, 46 South street
Andrews Thomas, photographer, 7 Cornmarket
Ashplant, Stapleton & Co. manure mers. 14 High street
Ashplant William Gilbert, agricultural chemical analyst & implement & manure merchant; office & laboratory, High street; stores, Cattle market
Ashton Seline (Mrs.), Old inn, Well street
Ayre John, Torridge inn, Mill street
Barrow Walter Philip, jeweller & engraver, South street
Beavan James Riley M.I.L.S. solicitor, clerk to the borough magistrates, clerk to the Great Torrington Commons Conservators, steward to Town Alms Land Trustees, solicitor to the North Devon Freehold Land Society & to the National Deposit Friendly Society (Devon Division) & clerk to the feoffees of parish lands of Shebbear, Potacre street
Bell Jane (Mrs.), photographic artist, 4 South street
Bennett William, registrar of marriages for Torrington dist. & sec. of Gt. Torrington Buildings Co. 25 Castle st
Blatchford George & Henry, saddlers & harness makers, 4 Potacre street
Blatchford Henry, boot & shoe dealer, tobacconist, & agent for Devon & Exeter Savings Bank & deputy registrar of births & deaths, Great Torrington sub-district, High st
Boatfield Frank R. manager of Fox, Fowler & Co.'s Bank & treasurer to the union, Fore street
Bowden Edward, tailor, New street
Bower Bessie (Mrs.), music dealer, Fore street
Bray James A. family draper, milliner & dress maker, agent for "C. B." corsets & for London Chemical Cleaning & Dyeing Co. High street
Buchanan Capt. Charles Griffiths, superintendent of the County police & inspector under the Contagious Diseases (Animals) & Food & Drug Acts, Court house
Burnett Capt. William Gordon, sub-steward to the Hon. Mark George Kerr Rolle, Little Silver
Cemetery (George Mark Doe, town clerk), Castle street
Chamier Edwin Francis M.A. steward to the Hon. Mark George Kerr Rolle, Little Silver
Chapple N., G. & M. chamois leather manufrs. Calf street
Clare Harriet A. (Miss), draper, South street
Clarke Henry, tailor & draper, Corn Market street
Clews John William, general draper, Well street
Cock John, boot & shoe maker, Well street
Collins Augustus & Son, watch & clock mas. 13 Fore st
Conservative Working Men's Association, Library & Reading Room (Lieut.-Col. Arthur Sutherland Macartney, hon. sec.), South street
Coombe Thomas, cabinet maker, New street
Cooper Frederick & Co. linen collar manufacturers, Well st
Co-operative Stores Limited, South street
Copp George Davey, general carrier, mourning coaches & carriages; furniture removed & agent to the London & South Western railway; omnibuses meet all trains, New street. See advertisement
Copp George, general printer, South street
Copp George Davey, auctioneer, valuer & insurance agent, certified bailiff under the "Law of Distress Amendment Act, 1888"; auction sales of stock held last saturday in the month, New street
Copp Thomas, farmer, Moortown
Cudmore William, jobbing gardener, Mill street
Cottage Hospital (Miss Julia Whiles, resident nurse; G. M. Doe, hon. sec. & treasurer), New street
Davey William, cowkeeper, Calf street
Davies William, draper & milliner, 13 Fore street & 12 Potacre street
Devon & Cornwall Banking Co. Limited (branch) (Reginald D. James, High street, manager); draw on Barclay & Co. Limited, London E C
Devon & Exeter Savings Bank (Henry Blatchford, agent), High street

Doe C. R. & R. M. wine & spirit merchants, South street
Doe George Mark, solicitor & commissioner for oaths, town clerk, clerk to the county magistrates, to Great Torrington school board, Torrington Rural District Council for Sanitary Purposes & registrar of the county court & acting high bailiff, vestry clerk & clerk to the guardians & assessment & school attendance committees of Torrington union & supt. registrar of Torrington district, 25 Castle street
Doidge George W. sec. to Gt. Torrington Gas Co. South st
Doidge Samuel, boys' school, Middle school, South street
Dyer Thomas John, printer & stationer, 8 Fore street
Dymond Thomas, apartments, Halsdon terrace
Easterbrook John, fly proprietor, Calf street
Eastmond Robert & Son, ironmongers, Fore street
Ebsary Richard, tailor, 1 Well street
Eddy Charles, fishmonger, New street
Elsworthy Thomas Tucker, hair dresser,High st. & Fore st
Endall Thomas, teacher of violin, Mill street
Fairchild Joshua, agent for Law Fire & the Edinburgh Life Insurance societies, 23 Castle street
Fairchild Thomas B. highway surveyor to the Great Torrington Rural District Council & sec. to the Great Torrington Agricultural Society, 2 New street
Fenwick William H. insurance agent, New street
Fishley Herman Edwin, dairyman, New street
Folland John, bailiff under the "Law of Distress Amendment Act, 1888" & bailiff of county court, New street
Folley John, mason, Well street
Forbes Henry, manager National Provincial Bank of England, High street
Fowler Thomas, postmaster & organist, Fore street
Fowler William, fly proprietor, New street
Fox Fowler & Co. bankers (branch) (Frank R. Boatfield, manager), Fore street; draw on Barclay & Co. Limited, London E C
Free Institute (William Vaughan, treasurer; Samuel Doidge, hon. sec.), Halsdon terrace
Friend John, ironmonger, South street
Friend Sydney, shopkeeper, 118 New street
Fry Roger, plumber, New street
Furse Thomas, Black Swan P.H. Potacre street
Gas Light & Coke Co. Lim. (George W. Dridge, sec)
Gerrard Frank, Plough inn, Fore street
Gilbert William, market gardener, Mill street
Gomer William, sanitary inspector to Urban District Council, Town hall
Grant Henry, builder & collector of assessed property & income taxes, Well street & South street
Great Torrington Agricultural Society (T. B. Fairchild, sec.), 2 New street
Great Torrington Bowling Club (Henry Slee esq. president; Henry Blatchford, hon. sec.), Fore street
Great Torrington Buildings Co. Limited (W. Bennett, sec.); registered office, Castle street
Griffits Mildred (Mrs.), chemist & druggist, 5 Fore street
Hackwill George H. Globe family & commercial hotel & posting in all its branches; good commercial, coffee & stock rooms; billiards; omnibus meets all trains; free fishing & shooting for visitors; golf links near, Fore st
Handford Edwin & Son, chemists, & stamp office, High st
Heard Silas & Sons, blacksmiths, New road
Herniman & Co. carriage builders, Calf street
Herring Mary E.& E. D.(Misses), girls' school,Halsdon ter
Heywood & Hodge (late Ashplant), wholesale & retail furnishing ironmongers, steel, bar iron, oil & color merchants & boot closed upper merchants, High street
Heywood William, wheelwright, White's lane
Hill Henry, grocer & provision dealer, Mill street
Hoare Margaret (Miss), shopkeeper, South street
Hookway Thomas, farmer, Bunwood
Hooper Ellen L. (Miss), bookseller & stationer, 9 Corn Market street
How John & Co. coal, manure & timber mers. Station; & at Bideford

Husband Margaret (Miss), clothier & boot & shoe dealer, High street
Hutchins Charles, agent Prudential Insurance Co. Well st
Isaac Richard, boot maker, 107 New street
Jackson John, glove & athletic goods manufr. New street
James Beaumont Tice, solicitor (attends saturdays), High street ; & at Barnstaple
James Reginald D. manager Devon & Cornwall Banking Co. Limited, High street
Jeffery Henry, farmer, Hill farm
Jenkins Joseph, New inn, Well street
Jones Wm. Joseph, Black Horse P.H. & coal dlr. High st
Judd Paul, shopkeeper, 10 Potacre street
Kingdon Elizabeth & Hannah (Misses), boarding & day school, Castle street
Lake William, farmer, Beam
Langbridge William & Son, plumbers & plaziers, New st
Langbridge Emma Nora (Mrs.), ironmonger, Well street
Langmead Albert Frederick, baker, Well street
Laver George William, New Market inn, South street
Lee Catherine (Mrs.), china & glass dealer, 16 South street
Lee John Bartlett, cabinet maker & collector of borough rates, South street
Lile John, grocer, South street
Livingstone Jas. Jn. inland revenue officer, 3 Queen's ter
Lloyd Squadron-Sergt.-Major Frederick, drill instructor to the A squadron Imperial Yeomanry & school attendance officer, 80 New street
Luxton Grace (Mrs.), baker, South street
Macindoe James Gray M.B., C.M. surgeon, New street
Martin Elizh. (Miss), apartments, Arlington cot. New st
Martin James, jun. farmer, Wood house
Martins Martin, boot & shoe dealer, South street
Masonic Lodge (Torridge No. 1885), held at Church yard second monday in every month (J. H. Sillifant, sec)
Medland William Cock, architect & surveyor & borough & town lands charity surveyor, sec. North Devon Freehold Land Society, agent to Sun Insurance Co. Windy cross
Millman Thomas R. temperance hotel ; good accommodation for commercials & visitors ; jobmaster, good stabling ; wholesale & retail game dealer, agent for cattle feeding cakes & potato merchant, High street
Moase John, farmer, Holland farm
Moore Robert, butcher, Well street
Morse Edward L.R.C.P. & S.Edin. surgeon, & medical officer High Bickington district, certifying factory surgeon & medical officer of health for borough of Torrington, South street
Mullins William, insurance agent, 215 New road
Muxworthy Richard, blacksmith, Calf street
Nation Eliza (Miss), grocer, Corn Market street
National Provincial Bank of England Limited (branch) (Henry Forbes, manager), High street ; draw on head office, 112 Bishopsgate within, London E C
National Society for the Prevention of Cruelty to Children (Miss K. Vaughan, sec), Castle street
Nethercott Elizabeth (Mrs.), greengrocer, High street
Netherton John Stocker, ironmonger, 5 Well street
Norman William, sexton & cemetery keeper, New street
North Devon Clay Co. Limited, clay miners & merchants & brick makers (Henry Holwill, manager), Marland brick works ; office, South street
North Devon Freehold Land Society (William Cock Medland, sec.) ; office, Windy cross (Norman H. Matthews, solicitor, South street)
North Devon Friendly Institution(Wm.Smale, agt.),New st
Palmer Lionel W. general posting stables ; carriages, wagonettes &c. for hire ; posting in all its branches, Church lane
Parnacott John, sculptor, stone & monumental mason; head stones in marble, granite, Forest of Dean & Portland stone & slate, 26 New street
Passmore William, hay & straw dealer, Well street
Pearce William, grocer, tea dealer & provision merchant, 2 High street & 179 New street
Penhale Richard E. L. M.R.C.V.S.Lond. veterinary surgeon, New street
Perkins William Harry, grocer & baker & agent for W. & A. Gilbey Limited, wine & spirit merchants, South st
Pettle James & Silas, farmers, Weeke
Phillips William, farmer, Darracott
Piper Thomas, decorator, Well street
Pope William, machinist, High street
Popham John, baker, Well street
Pow & Parkhouse, basket makers, Calf street
Prouse James, tanner &c. Church lane
Reddaway Isaac, butcher, Well street
Reed John B. farmer, wool, seed, corn, manure & coal merchant & lime burner, Staple vale & South street
Reed William Henry, farmer, Furse

Richards Arthur Edwin, Setting Sun P.H. Cornmarket st
Rockey Thomas, carpenter, Calf street
Rodd Albert William, thatcher, New street
Rowe Jn. Passmore, watch & clock maker, Corn Market st
Royal North Devon Imperial Yeomanry (Hussars) (A Squadron, Capt. & Hon. Major H. H. J. W. Drummond, commanding ; Capt. J. Bayly, second in command ; William Tanton, squadron quarter-master; Squadron-Sergt.-Major Frederick Lloyd, drill instructor), 80 New street
Rudd Lucy A. (Mrs.), silk glove manufacturer, New st
Rude John, ale & porter merchant, 8 Potacre street
St. Giles-in-the-Wood Female Friendly Society (Frederick Copp, sec.), Well street
Sanders Mary W. (Miss), dress maker, New street
Sandford Robert & Son, seed merchants, High street
Sandford Thomas, market gardener, Mill street
Sandford William Henry, seedsman, fruiterer & greengrocer, High street
Short & Son, tailors, Castle street
Short George & Joseph, tailors & outfitters, Fore street
Short Gertrude (Miss), Railway hotel, New street
Short John, boot maker & town crier & bill poster, New st
Sillifant Alfred, jun. butcher, 4 Fore street
Sillifant Alfred, sen. butcher, New street
Skemp Emma (Mrs.), fishing tackle manufr. South street
Slee Charles Herbert, seed mer. & butcher, 12 South st
Slee Henry (F.A.I.) & Sons, auctioneers, valuers & estate agents ; auction sales of stock held on the last saturday in every month & fortnightly during the summer months ; offices, South street
Slee Joseph John, cabinet maker & carpenter, New street
Smale William, deputy registrar of marriages, Kempton cottage, New street
Snow R. M. & Co. wholesale grocers, South street
Squire Elias Edmund, agricultural seed merchant ; district representative for W. O. Smith & Co.'s pure cakes & manures ; office & stores,
Squire John, tailor & woollen draper, 3 & 5 South street
Stamp Office (Edwin Handford, sub-distributor), High st
Stanbury William, farmer, Norwood
Stapleton & Sons, bakers & confectioners, The Machine Bakery, Fore street
Stapleton Wm. manure mer. see Ashplant, Stapleton & Co
Stawell George, solicitor, Mill street
Steevenson Robert H. card box maker, Well street
Stevens John Henry, hair dresser, 6 South street
Stevenstone Fox Hounds, Kennels, Rotherham bridge
Sutcliff Edward Harvey M.B.Durh., M.R.C.S.Eng., L.R.C.P.Lond. surgeon & medical officer & public vaccinator for Torrington district, Park villa
Tanton J. & Son, grocers & bakers, Well street
Tanton William E. relieving officer No. 1 district & registrar of births & deaths & vaccination & school attendance officer, Great Torrington sub-district, 219 New street
Tapscott James, apartments, Grenville house
Tavener Henry, shopkeeper, Calf street
Thorne Thomas, shoe maker, Well street
Torridge Vale Butter Factory (Robert Sandford & Son, proprietors)
Torrington Fire Brigade (William Heywood, captain)
Torrington United Tradesmen's Sick & Burial Society (Charles Booth, jun. sec.), New street
Town Hall (John D. Copp, keeper), High street
Trott George, shoe maker, Corn Market street
Tucker Frederick, baker, 125 New street
Turrall William Henry, stationer, bookseller, printer & Sutton's agent, High street
Twiggs John & Sons, wholesale marine store & toy & china dealers & wool staplers, 6 Potacre street
United Tradesmen's Sick & Burial Society (William Langbridge, sec.), New street
Union Female Society, held at Black Horse (T.Winson, sec)
Vaughan William, silk glove maker, White's lane
Volunteer Battalion (4th) Devonshire Regiment (F Company, Capt. H. D. F. Pollock ; Color-Sergt. E. Hooper, drill instructor), Drill hall & armoury, Calf street ; orderly room, Town hall
Walkey Mary B. (Mrs.), Royal Exchange inn, New street
Ward Frederick & Sons, basket makers, New street
Ward John, carpenter & joiner, Mill street
Warren John, Hunter's inn, Well street
Watkins Albert, cattle dealer
Watkins Edward, cattle dealer
Watts Henry, saddler & boot dealer, Corn Market street
Webber Silvanus, draper & milliner, High street
Westcott Eliza (Mrs.), shopkeeper, Well street
Yeo Brothers, farmers, Priestacott
Yeo Elizabeth (Mrs.), furnished apartments, 130 New st
Yeo Thomas, farmer, Coombe farm

Castle Street and the fire-engine. Note the early cinema poster on the right.

The Torrington fire brigade in the 1890s.

Sydney House, South Street. This was built by Mr Vaughan in 1887, at a cost of £10,000. He was mayor of Torrington in 1884–86 and 1897–99. Sydney House was used as a hospital in the First World War, and subsequently as a children's home. It burnt down on 19 February 1942, with the loss of five children's lives. It is now the site of the South Street Car Park.

Jack Gilbert (with the barrel), brewer, at the Plough Inn, with some of his customers, c. 1900.

The customers lined up outside the Setting Sun, possibly on a market day.

Ford & Lock's Christmas window, 1907.

The Wesleyan Chapel.

Carnival Tableau, c. 1910. Thomas Evans, Harry Nicholls, Harry Walkley, Arthur Tuckett, R. Good, Richard Guard, Richard Furzeman, Tom Heywood, Syd Lake, Walter Piper (of No. 57 Well Street).

View of the square and the Black Horse Inn. William Cory had this photograph taken between 1873 and 1876.

TADDIPORT is a hamlet, 1½ miles north, on the south bank of the river Torridge, which is here crossed by a bridge of three arches, leading to Torrington.

The hospital of St. Mary Magdalen, founded here about the 13th century, was given in 1665 by Tristram Arscott esq. to Great Torrington and the churchwardens of Little Torrington for the relief of the poor, and the lands now known as "Magdalen Lands" were anciently part of the endowment of this hospital, which was originally a lazar-house, or asylum for lepers; these lands now consist of two fields, comprising 8 acres, several gardens and 13 cottages, let for about £34 yearly.

The chapel of St. Mary Magdalen, formerly attached to the hospital, was founded by the ancestors of John Sentleger (St. Leger) in 1345, and is a small building about 39 feet in length by 11 feet wide, with a transept, and a western tower 5 feet square, containing one bell, dated 1654: a new east window has been placed in the chapel, but one of the old windows with wooden tracery lingers still. Divine service is held here once or twice on sundays. There is an endowment towards the maintenance of the chapel and its services of £12 5s. per annum, this endowment forming a part of the Magdalen charity, the residue of which is distributed among the poor of Great and Little Torrington.

Hart's charity of £7 is distributed to the poor at Christmas by four trustees.

Schools.

National (mixed), built in 1840 & enlarged in 1873, for 70 children; average attendance, 50; Mrs. A. Cottle, mistress

A milk lorry loaded with churns going through the floods at Taddiport, 14 January 1955.

SATTERLEIGH and WARKLEIGH form a parish, settled under the provisions of the "Local Government Act, 1888," by an order of the County Council, dated 2nd Aug. 1894, uniting the parish of Satterleigh to that of Warkleigh, the united parishes being called Satterleigh and Warkleigh. This order was confirmed by the Local Government Board 21st Nov. 1894, and from and after the 17th Dec. in that year the two parishes were so united. The part of the parish known as Warkleigh, is on the river Taw, 4½ miles east from Umberleigh station and 4 north from Portsmouth Arms station, both on the North Devon branch of the London and South Western railway, 5 south-west from South Molton and 10 south-east from Barnstaple,

The Boundy family.

WARKLEGH.
(Marked thus * receive letters thro' Chulmleigh.)
*Owen William, Higher Watertown
Mortimer Samuel, Warkleigh Barton
Thorold Mrs. Warkleigh house
Thorold Rev. John Leofric de Buckenhold M.A. The Rectory
COMMERCIAL.
*Baker John, farm bailiff to William Owen esq. Higher Watertown
Beer James, thatcher, Deason
Beer William, thatcher, Deason
*Elston John, farmer, The Hermitage
Greenslade William, farmr.Stonehayes
Herniman Robert, farmer, Claytown
Huxtable Edwin,frmr.Old Parsonage
Lew Mary Ann (Miss), frmr. Hilltwn
Mortimer Sml.farmr.WarkleighBartn
Robinson Edward, schoolmaster & assistant overseer
Rodd John, farmer, Deason
*Russell Herbert, dairyman,Woodlgh
*Saunders Henry, shoe maker
Shapland Jas. farmer, Low.Greendwn
Simmons John, blacksmith
*Sing William, farmer. Newland
*Squire Saul. farmr. Low.Watertwn
*Townsend Eliza (Mrs.), farmer, Haynetown
Trick Emma (Mrs.), farmr. Broadmr
Tucker Henry, farmer, Pugsley
*Turner John Wm. dairy, Hill's
Westacott William, farmer, Holt gate

Woolsery (Black Dog) Board School, c. 1904. The master was Mr Rogers.

WASHFORD PYNE is a small parish and scattered village, 9 miles north from Crediton station and 7 north-east from Morchard Road station on the North Devon branch of the London and South Western railway, in the Northern division of the county, hundred of Witheridge, Crediton petty sessional division, union and county court district, rural deanery of West Tiverton, and archdeaconry and diocese of Exeter. The church of St. Peter is an edifice of stone in the Decorated style, rebuilt in 1883-5 at a cost of about £1,246, and consists of chancel, nave, south porch and a western tower, with tiled steeple, containing 3 bells, dated respectively 1787, 1620 and 1731: the chancel was rebuilt in 1887: the carved oak lectern was executed and presented by Mrs. Jenkins, sister of the patron: there are 75 sittings. The register of baptisms and burials dates from the year 1587; marriages, 1746. The living is a rectory, net yearly value £120, including 156 acres of glebe, with residence, in the gift of C. Comyns Tucker esq. and held since 1899 by the Rev. Cecil Charles Robert Tyndall B.A. of University College, Durham. At Wonham are some ancient remains, possibly monastic, and including a window built into a shed in a farm-yard. There was also once a chapel here. C. Comyns Tucker esq. of Morchard Bishop, is lord of the manor and chief landowner. Messrs. John and William Bragg and John T. Leach esq. have estates in the parish. The soil is loam and clay, and the subsoil is clay. The chief crops are wheat and oats and some pasture land. The acreage is 1,144; rateable value, £712; the population in 1891 was 141.

HIGHER and LOWER BLACK DOG are hamlets, 1½ miles west and 1 south from Witheridge

Sexton, Mrs. Faith Willis.

Post & M. O. O., S. B. & Annuity & Insurance Office, Black Dog.—William Bradford, sub-postmaster. Letters through Morchard Bishop R.S.O. North Devon, arrive at 5.55 a.m.; dispatched at 7.25 p.m. Morchard Bishop, 3 miles distant, is the nearest telegraph office

Wall Letter Box, near the Church, cleared at 6.30 p.m. except sundays

Washford Pyne is included in the Woolfardisworthy, Washford Pyne & Kennerleigh United School Board district, formed May 3, 1876

Board School, Black Dog (mixed), erected in 1878, & enlarged in 1900, for 120 children; average attendance, 85; for the parishes of Kennerleigh, Thelbridge, Washford Pyne & Woolsery; William Henry Rogers, master; Mrs. Jane Rogers, mistress

Carrier to Exeter.—Thomas Tidball, from Witheridge, passes through thurs. returning fri

West Emlett Farm which was destroyed by fire.

WASHFORD PYNE.

Tyndall Rev. Cecil Charles Robert B.A. (rector)

Southcott Hy.mllr.(water),Pensfrd.ml
Sturgess Samuel, mason
Webber Frederick, dairyman, Pyne

Bragg John, farmer, Wonham
Couch Emmnl. drymn. Low. Gate ho
Leach Jn. T. frmr. & lndownr.Copstn
Lock Samuel, farmer, HigherGate ho

BLACK DOG.

Bradford Wm. whlwrght. & postmastr
Chapple Fredk. tailor & asst. oversr

Matthews George, farmer, Henciford
Radford Wm. dairyman, Town close
Searle William, blacksmith
Selley Geo. farmer, Washford Barton

Cobley Wm. Black Dog P.H. & farmr
Dayment Henry, blacksmith

The Blackford family of Westcott Farm, Thelbridge, c. 1909. Lily, Tom, Elsie (with basket) and Fred (nearest camera). These children would have been pupils at The Black Dog Board School (see p. 138).

THELBRIDGE is a parish and village on the road from Crediton to South Molton, 5 miles north-east from Lapford station on the North Devon branch of the London and South Western railway, 9 north-north-west from Crediton, 7 east-south-east from Chulmleigh and 15 north-west from Exeter, in the Northern division of the county, Witheridge hundred, South Molton petty sessional division, Crediton union and county court district, rural deanery of Chulmleigh, archdeaconry of Barnstaple and diocese of Exeter. The church of St. David is a small building of stone in the Early English style, consisting of chancel, nave, south porch and an embattled western tower with pinnacles containing 6 bells: in the church is a tablet to the Rev. Robert Venn, sometime rector here, who died in 1689, and is mentioned in Fox's "Sufferings of the Clergy": the stained east window was presented by the parishioners in 1872, in which year the church was thoroughly restored at a cost of £650, and has 150 sittings. The register dates from about 1612. The living is a rectory, net yearly value £178, with 149 acres of glebe valued at £110, and residence, in the gift of and held since 1893 by the Rev. John Hill. Hosegood M.A. of Jesus College, Cambridge. The poor have £3 13s. yearly distributed at Easter. Frederick Maunder esq. is lord of the manor. The rector and Messrs. Maunder are the principal landowners, and there are several freeholders. The soil is loam; subsoil, clay. The chief crops are wheat, barley and oats. The area is 4,006 acres; rateable value, £2,599; the population in 1901 was 319.

By Local Government Board Order, 16,343, a detached part of Witheridge, in South Molton union, was added to this parish, March 25, 1885.

Letters from Morchard Bishop R.S.O. arrive at 6.30 a.m. The nearest money order & telegraph office is at Witheridge, 3 miles distant. Wall Letter Box cleared at 7.10 p.m

This place was made contributory to the Woolfordisworthy United District School board, June 30, 1876, sending two members

The children attend the Board school at Black Dog

Adams Mrs. Providence villa
Blake George, Woodhouse villa
Hosegood Rev. Jn. Hill M.A. Rectory
Mitchell Thomas, Providence villa

COMMERCIAL.

Arscott Edwin, farmer, Eastway
Arscott Frederick, farmer, Mill
Blackford William, farmer, Westcott
Crang Daniel, farmer, Upcott
Davey Allan, farmer, Charnaford

Davies Joseph, farmer, Stourton
Down Charles, farmer, New house
Fisher Matthew, farmer, Woodington
Harris John, farmer, Buddleswick
Hill William, farmer, Woodhouse
Hooper Rowland, farmer, Higher & Lower Somerville
Leach John Torrington, Thelbridge inn & farmer
Loosemore John, shopkeeper
Matthew George, farmer, Henciford

Maunder Frederick James Partridge, yeoman, Middlewick
Maunder John, farmer, Ludon
May Philip, farmer, Marchweek
Partridge Elias, farmer, Woodford Mill barn
Selley William, farmer, Westway
Slater William, farmer, Woodford
Tucker Daniel, farmer, Hele Barton
Tucker Fras. Edwd. yeoman, Chapner

WEAR GIFFORD is a parish on the river Torridge, 3½ miles south from Bideford station on the Torrington branch of the London and South Western railway, 3 north-west from Torrington, in the Northern division of the county, Shebbear hundred, Torrington petty sessional division, union and county court district, rural deanery of Hartland, archdeaconry of Barnstaple and diocese of Exeter. The church of the Holy Trinity is an edifice of stone in the Decorated style, consisting of chancel, nave, south aisle, south porch and an embattled western tower, with pinnacles, containing 6 bells, five of which were cast in 1765 by Thomas Bilbie, of Cullompton: the chancel has a fine roof of Perpendicular date: in the north wall of the nave, within two recessed arches, are two recumbent effigies of a cross-legged knight and a lady; the former, placed on a white altar-tomb, is in a suit of mail, with cowl, covered by a cyclas, or long-skirted tunic, and carries a shield and sword; the figure of the lady wears a coronet, and is attired in whimple and flowing robes, covered by a mantle, and at the sides are mutilated figures of angels holding up drapery; these effigies may represent Sir Walter Giffard, lord of this place in 1243, and his wife: there are also memorials to the Fortescues, and a modern brass: the church was thoroughly restored and reseated and a new tenor bell hung in 1869: there are 300 sittings. The register dates from the year 1583. The living is a rectory, net yearly value £118, including 5½ acres of glebe, with residence, in the gift of Viscount Ebrington, and held since 1891 by the Rev. Stephen Wade M.A. of Balliol College, Oxford. Here are Wesleyan chapels. John Lovering's charity, amounting to £10 3s. 8d. yearly, is distributed in money. The country is finely wooded and fish are abundant in the river Torridge. Wear Hall, belonging to the Fortescue family, is an interesting structure of the 15th century, consisting of a central block with wings, occupied for some time as a farmhouse, but restored in 1832 by the late Hon. George Fortescue: the embattled gatehouse remains, and the dining hall, a noble apartment, 19ft. by 33ft. has fine carved oak panelling and a beautifully carved oak roof: other portions of the mansion retain similar work and some ancient portraits and tapestry: it is now occupied by His Honor Judge Cecil Hugh Wriothesley Beresford B.A., J.P. judge of Circuit No. 28. This place takes its name from the Giffard family, who held the manor during several centuries: in the reign of Henry VI. it passed by marriage to Martin, son of Sir John Fortescue, Lord High Chancellor, from whom it has descended to its present owner, Earl Fortescue. Viscount Ebrington, who is lord of the manor, the Hon. Mark George Kerr Rolle, and the Rev. Richard Turner M.A. vicar of West Bickleigh, are the chief landowners. The soil is good loam; subsoil, clay. The chief crops are wheat, barley and oats. The area is 1,703 acres of land, 2 of water, 20 of tidal water and 12 of foreshore; rateable value, £1,898; the population in 1901 was 299.

Parish Clerk, John Clarke, jun.

MILL HOUSE, WEARE GIFFARD, BIDEFORD.

Mill House, Weare Giffard.

The old post office.

Post Office.—John Gomer, sub-postmaster. Letters received from Bideford at 9 a.m. ; dispatched at 4.55 p.m. week days only. Postal orders are issued here, but not paid. The nearest money order & telegraph office is at Torrington, 3 miles distant

Wall Letter Box, Rectory wall, cleared at 5.15 p.m. week days only

National (Endowed) School (mixed), erected in 1860, & having an endowment of £20, invested in Consols, left by John Lovering in 1671; it will hold 80 children; average attendance about 50; J. M. Tucker, master

Police Station, Emanuel Blackmore, constable

PRIVATE RESIDENTS.

Balsdon Mrs. Ingleside
Beresford His Honor Judge Cecil Hugh Wriothesley B.A.,J.P. Wear hall
Bickford Col. William, The Cottage
Cooper J. Groves, The Hill
Cooper Miss, Pine wood
Fernie Miss
Fry Thomas, Mill house
Johnstone Mrs. Hazel cottage
Meeking Thos. Arth. Road Cliff cot

Wade Rev. Stephen M.A. Rectory

COMMERCIAL.

Balsdon Robert Percy, frmr.WearBrtn
Blackmore Emanuel, police constable
Braddon William, hind to William Hy. Turner esq. Huxhill
Bright James, shoe maker
Bright Wm. carpenter & shopkeeper
Channings William, frmr. Little Wear
Clarke John, jun. carpenter & sexton

Ellis Ann (Mrs.), farmer, Saltrens
Fry T. & Co. millers (water),Wear mill
Gomer John, mason, Post office
Grigg Thomas, farmer, Netherdown
Lovering George, farmer, Venton
Martin Edwd. frmr. Southcott Barton
Perkin Robert, carter
Short William Henry, farmer, Brookham farm
Westlake William, carpenter
Wilton Thomas, farmer, Cleave

Children playing at Chopes Bridge.

Weare Giffard Hall.

The shop, and beyond it the greenhouse and old barn, in the garden of Brookham Farm. In 1970 Brookham, then owned by Mr and Mrs Yates and family, was turned into a public house. John Yates, the first licencee, called the pub the Cyder Press because there had once been a cider press in the barn, and it was reputed that more men gathered there to drink scrumpy on Sunday mornings than the vicar at that time had in his congregation.

The Mill House Tea Room. Weare Giffard is famous for its strawberries, and many a luscious cream tea must have been served on this lawn in idyllic surroundings.

Riversdale Farm, part of which now houses the post office, and which for many years was the home of John and Lucy Moore, and their sons, Robert, David, Charles, and their sister Jean.

Weare Giffard School, 1928. From left to right: Ernie Becklake, Jimmy Martin, Frank Wilton, Alfie Tanton, Arthur Edworthy, Wallace Mackenzie, Sonny Braunton, Harold Edworthy, Joan Moore, Joan Mancey, Phyllis Braunton, Elsie Beer, Margery Beer, Marjorie Gilbert, Hilda Braunton, Vera Beer, Evaline Beer, Jack Braunton, George Gorvett, Dulcie Edworthy, Clara Becklaker, Violet Curtis, Gwen Braunton, Vera Braunton, Aubrey Braunton.

The School – now become the Village Hall.

The Weare Giffard Home Guard in 1940.

The Choir. Could I have some names for these two photographs please?

Little Weare Barton, c. 1905.

The manor house and church tower, Weare Giffard.

WINKLEIGH is a parish and ancient village on the road from Crediton to Torrington, 4 miles south-west from Eggesford station on the North Devon branch and 5 miles north-west from North Tawton station on the Devon and Cornwall section of the London and South Western railway, 6 south-west from Chulmleigh, 12 south-east from Torrington and 22 west-north-west from Exeter, in the Northern division of the county, North Tawton and Winkleigh hundred, South Molton petty sessional division, Torrington union and county court district, rural deanery of Chulmleigh, archdeaconry of Barnstaple and diocese of Exeter. The church of All Saints is an ancient building of stone, chiefly in the Late Decorated style, and consists of chancel, nave, north aisle, south porch, transept and an embattled western tower with pinnacles, containing a clock with chimes, presented by Miss R. Pinckard, and 8 bells: the chancel and nave are separated from the north aisle by an arcade of six arches, supported on clustered columns: the trefoiled piscina, with its projecting basin, is of Decorated date, and the ancient priest's door on the south side still remains: the windows of the nave and aisle are of Perpendicular character, but many of them have been restored: the reredos, of alabaster and mosaics, presented by Sir Charles Turner K.C.B. in memory of his parents, at a cost of £150, was designed by the late Mr. J. Gould, architect; the carved work was carried out by Mr. Harry Hems, of Exeter: the pulpit was presented by Mrs. Letheren, the organ by Mrs. Henry Pinckard, and the lectern by Miss Hartridge: in 1873 the church underwent a thorough restoration, at an expense of nearly £7,000, through the munificence of G. H. Pinckard esq. of Combe Court, Godalming, Surrey: there are 400 sittings. The register of baptisms dates from the year 1585; marriages and burials, 1569. The living is a vicarage, net yearly value £207, with residence and 9 acres of glebe, in the gift of the Dean and Chapter of Exeter, and held since 1887 by the Rev. Henry Bremridge M.A. of St. John's College, Oxford, rural dean of Chulmleigh, and surrogate. The Rev. William Davey, vicar of this place and some time curate of Lustleigh, who died in 1826, wrote and printed with his own hands "A System of Divinity in 26 Volumes," 14 copies only being completed. A mission church, dedicated to St. Michael and All Angels, was erected at Hollacombe in 1891, at a cost of £900: the building is of local stone, in the Early English style, and consists of chancel, nave, vestry, porch and a tower: the stained central light of the east window was the gift of the parishioners in memory of the late Earl of Portsmouth, d. 1891; the windows on either side are memorials to the Rev. James Philip Bremridge M.A. vicar 1872-87, and his widow; services are held every Sunday. There are Wesleyan and Bible Christian chapels in the village, a Bible Christian chapel at Stable Green and a Congregational chapel at Hollacombe, erected in 1869. The church lands have been applied to the repair of the church from an early period, and comprise an undivided moiety of a farm, called East Chapple. The poor parishioners have £2 12s. yearly from Sir John Acland's charity and the interest of £30 left by unknown donors. A sum of money left by Mr. John Ashplant, the Skinner Charity and the Gidleigh Charity produce about £6 yearly, which is distributed among poor widows over 60 years of age.

High Street, 1906.

South Street.

The villagers going on an outing. Carters Commercial Hotel is on the right.

PRIVATE RESIDENTS.

Bremridge Rev. Henry M.A. (vicar, rural dean & surrogate), Vicarage
Bremridge Philip, Linden house
Crosthwaite Sir Robt. Joseph K.C.S.I., B.A. Winkleigh court
*Davie Philip, Ashley cottage
Davis Alexander, Seckington
Dulling Mrs. Castle street
Dunning Major Richard Horwood J.P. Hilliers
Ford Miss, Heath cottage
Godwin Mrs. The Cottage
Heysham Mrs. The Parsonage
Norman James Henry, Goodleigh
Scott Rev. Montague B.A. (curate), Ward mill
*Whiteford Rev. Charles (Cong.), Hollacombe

COMMERCIAL.

Ashplant Chas. farmer & shopkeeper
*Babbage James, farmer, Babbages
Baker John, farmer, Herdwick
Baker John, jun. carpenter
Bartlett Albert, watch & clock maker
*Bird John, boot maker, Hollacombe
Boundy Richard, farmer, Garradown
Brook Theodore, tailor
*Brook Thomas, mason, Hollacombe
*Brook Wm. blacksmith, Hollacombe
*Brook William, mason, Hollacombe
Chambers William, wheelwright & farmer, Wood Roberts
Chamings Albt.W. farmer, Heckapen
*Cole James, farmer, Nrth. Collacott
Cole Richard, farmer, Bidbere (letters through North Tawton)
Cole Richard, farmer, East heath
*Cole William, farmer, West Ashley
Collihole Thos. grocer & ironmonger
Coombe William, rope & twine maker
*Cowle John, farmer, Bransgrove
Cowle William, farmer, Wood Terrell
Crocker Josiah, tailor
*Darch James, miller (water) & farmer. Horry mill
*Davie William, farmer, East Ashley
Devon & Cornwall Banking Co. Lim. (sub-branch) (James Letheren, agent), open mon. 10 to 11 a.m. ; fri. 4 to 5 p.m. ; draw on Barclay & Co. Limited, London E C

Davey John, farmer, Penson (letters through North Tawton)
Down George, farmer, Durdon
Down Thomas, farmer, Stabdon
Dulling Albert Edward, shopkeeper
Dulling James, tailor
Farleigh J. S. & Co. grocers, & agents for W. & A. Gilbey Limited, wine & spirit merchants
Francis Edward, watch & clock ma
Francis Henry, carpenter
Francis William, tinplate worker
Friend Mrs. Emily K. bookseller, stationer, fancy repository & Post off
Harris Joshua, farmer, Puncherdon
Harris Thos. farmer & miller (water) Taw mill
Hellyer John (Mrs.), farmer, Collacott
Heywood Thos. G. farmr. Ea.Chapple
Hill Charles, Winkleigh hotel, & agent for Goulding's manures & seed mer
Inch John, carpenter
Inch Samuel, carpenter
Isaac Ade Parkin, farmer, Crispin
Isaac Edmund James, farmer & cattle dealer, Townsend house
Isaac Ephraim,farmer, LoosedonBartn
Isaac Ephraim Batt, farmer, Chapel Downs
Isaac Frederick James, butcher & farmer, Clotworthy
Isaac Henry, game dealer & seed merchant, Park place
Jones William, shoeing & general smith
Lane Jabez, farmer, Whitehouse
Lendon Samuel, Barnstaple inn
Letheren Annie (Mrs.), draper
Letheren Frederick George, saddler
Letheren John, baker
Letheren Lucina (Miss), baker
Luxton Moses & Sons, agricultural implement makers
Luxton Robert, yeoman, Hill
Luxton Robt. Geo. farmer,Riddlestone (letters through North Tawton)
Luxton Robert John, farmer, Chapel
Manning William, farmer, Southcott
Miller Josiah, farmer, Gray's bridge
Mitchell Ann (Miss), dress maker
Mitchell Charles, carpenter
Mitchell John, blacksmith
Molland John, farmer, East Luxton (letters through North Tawton)
Molland William, jun. farmer, Lower Narracott (letters through Ashreigney, Chulmleigh)

*Molland Richd. wheelwrt.Hollacombe
Molland William, farmer, Park place
NewcombeWm.boot & shoe ma.Park pl
Norman James Henry L.R.C.P. & S. Edin. physician & surgeon & medical officer, Winkleigh district, Torrington union, Goodleigh
*Nott George, farmer, Pittaford
Paddon Bartholomew, farmer, Garraton & Higher & Lower Coulson
Paddon Thomas, farmer, Wheatland
Parker George, shoe maker
*Partridge William, farmer, Gosses
*Pickard Jonathan, farmer, Pensford
Potter George, farmer, Puncherdon
*Rattenbury Wm. farmer, Pensford
Rawle David, veterinary surgeon
Raymont John, farmer
Reading Room (Rev. H. Bremridge, hon. sec)
Reed John, earthenware dealer
*Rice Richard, farmer, Kingsland
Robbins George, mason
Saunders Edward, photographer, & temperance hotel
Saunders John, farmer,West Riddiford
Saunders Robert, farmer, Heath hill
Shopland John, farmer, Ward
Short Jonathan, yeoman, Westwood
*Sowden Fredk. farmer.New House fm
*Stevens Francis, farmer, Higher Hollacombe
Stevens Samuel, farmer, Park
Tinney Edward, Ring of Bells P.H
Tout William, farmer, Narracott (letters through Ashreigney, Chulmleigh)
Tucker Richard, shopkeeper
Turner William, King's Arms P.H
*Underhill Wm. farmr. Chittlehmptn
Wadland Thomas, farmer, Down
Westaway John, farmer, Week house
Westaway Richard, clerk to the Parish Council & assist. overseer,Week ho
*Westcott Henry, farmer, Smitham
Westcott Simon, farmer
*Weston Amos, farmer, Stable green
Winkleigh Hotel (Charles Hill, proprietor), 4 miles from Eggesford station ; first-class accommodation for visitors & cyclists, hot & cold baths, good shooting, golf links in adjoining parish, & within easy distance of meeting points of four packs of hounds
Woollacott Thos.blacksmith & carrier

Another view of Fore Street, 1911.

Farmworkers on Parsonage Farm: R. M., Harry Knight, R. Ware, Jack Knight, Luxton, Tom Lugg, W. Ware, Gilbert Lugg, Sid Jones, Jack Mitchell, C. Ware, Herbert Bearding, Tom Knight, Bill Coombe, Sam Inch, Bill Samson, Bert Parker. Unfortunately in which order these names go, or to which faces they belong is unknown.

Waiting at the pump. Water rationing in Winkleigh in 1921. Was this another very dry year, I wonder?

Saunders' grocery shop.

Mid Devon Motor Company's workshop. Edward Saunders is in the centre, the young boy is Mr Dulling, then aged 15.

WEST BUCKLAND is a parish and village, pleasantly seated on an acclivity, 2½ miles north from Filleigh station, on the Taunton and Barnstaple branch of the Great Western railway and 6 north-west from South Great Western railway, 6 north-west from South Molton and 8 east from Barnstaple, in the Northern division of the county, Braunton hundred, South Molton petty sessional division, union and county court district, rural deanery of South Molton, archdeaconry of Barnstaple and diocese of Exeter. The church of St. Peter is a building of stone in the Early English style, consisting of a chancel, nave, south aisle, south porch and a lofty embattled western tower containing 6 bells: the east window is stained: in the church are memorials of William Butterfield, d. 1777, and his wife, d. 1771: in the early part of the present century this church possessed an ornate and interesting screen, but on the rebuilding of the church it was taken down and not replaced, and in 1880, its then remaining fragments were incorporated in the screen of Swymbridge church: the church, with the exception of the tower, was entirely rebuilt about 1860, and affords 200 sittings. The register dates from the year 1684.

Schools.

The Devon County School stands on high ground, 650 feet above sea level, partly in this parish & partly in that of East Buckland: the school was founded in 1861 by the late Earl Fortescue & Prebendary Brereton, to provide a public school education for boys of the middle classes of this & the adjoining counties. The buildings, erected at a cost of £12,000, are adapted for the reception of nearly 200 boarders & attached are playing fields & shrubberies, covering about 24 acres. The late Earl Fortescue also gave £1,000 to endow a chaplain to the school, at the same time rebuilding & enlarging East Buckland church for the use of the boys; Wm. Arthur Knight M.A. head master; Adelbert Taylor, sec.; Rev. Ernest Charles Harries B.A. chaplain; Robert Heron Spear B.A. Adelbert Taylor & Henry Pickard, assistant masters

National (mixed), built in 1875, for 70 children; average attendance, 50; Samuel Weston, master; Mrs. Gertrude Weston, mistress

West Buckland School group, 1874.

A first XI old boys match in 1881.

Carrier.

Barnstaple.—James Holloway, tues. & fri. Angel inn

PRIVATE RESIDENTS.

George Murry Thorne, The Hutt
Harries Rev. Ernest Charles B.A.
  (chaplain), Devon County school
Knight William Arthur M.A. Devon
  County school
Laws Jeremiah
Newman Rev. Josiah M.A. Rectory
Newman Miss, Bay cottage
Pickard Henry, Devon County school
Spear Robert Heron B.A. Devon
  County school
Taylor Adelbert, Devon County schl

COMMERCIAL.

Bale William, tailor & draper
Balment George, gardener to Devon
  County school
Clatworthy John, blacksmith

Dallyn John, grocer, draper, shoeing
  & general smith, maker of all kinds
  agricultural implements & agent to
  National Deposit Friendly Society,
  Post office
Davey Alma (Mrs.), shopkeeper
Davey Wm. carpenter & wheelwright
Devon County School (Wm. Arthur
  Knight M.A. head master)
Down Richard Elias, farmer, Gubbs
Heywood Bartholomew, farmer,
  Bright's Leary
Holloway James, farmer & carrier
Huxtable Wm. Herbt. frmr. Middle hl
Manning Andrew, farmer, May's Leary
Manning Thomas, farmer, Hilliers
  Leary
Miller Thos. butcher & farmer, Leary

Miller William, farmer & butcher,
  Stoodley south
New Inn Public House Company
  (Charles Nott, manager)
Nott Lewis, farmer, Bushtown farm
Parker James, farmer, Indicombe
Rice Charles, wheelwright
Searle Samuel, thatcher
Shepherd Reginald, shoe maker
Skinner Frederick Alexander, farmr.
  Middle Stoodley
Skinner Thomas, farmer, Leary Bartn
Smallridge Fdk. farmer, Stoodley nth
Slape Brothers, farmers, Bucking-
  ham's, Leary
Thorne William, farmer, Furze
Vickery Alfred, farmer, Witsford
Yeo William, farmer, Home Barton

Masters and monitors, 1885.

Domestic staff group photograph, West Buckland, 1907.

WITHERIDGE is a parish and village on the road from South Molton to Tiverton, 7 miles north-east from Lapford station on the North Devon branch of the London and South Western railway, and about 8 south-east from Bishopsnympton station on the Barnstaple section of the Great Western railway, 10½ south-east from South Molton and 10½ west-by-north from Tiverton, in the Northern division of the county, Witheridge hundred, South Molton petty sessional division, union and county court district, and in the rural deanery of South Molton, archdeaconry of Barnstaple and diocese of Exeter.

PRIVATE RESIDENTS.

Adams William, The Square
Bennett Thomas, North street
Benson Rev. John Peter M.A. (vicar & rural dean), Vicarage
Benson Miss E. The Lawn
Charlton Thomas William, Colleton hall, Hill town
Cheney Rev. Henry (Congregational), The Manse
Cock George, Commercial cottage
Cutcliffe Mrs. Coombe house
Elworthy Mrs. Lashbrook
Fernie Miss, The Square
Folland Frank, Burn house
Holt Geo. Frederick, Lawn cottage
Partridge Mrs. Elizabeth, Fern cot
Partridge Mrs. Ellen, South street
Pullen Geo. Henry, sen. Rosemont vil
Shelley Percy Wilfred Graham M.R.C.S.Eng., L.R.C.P.Lond. Cypress house
Tucker Mrs. Fore street

Motor buses starting from Witheridge.

COMMERCIAL.

Adams Richard, dairyman, The Lawn
Adams Richard, farmer, Hole
Addicott Fanny (Mrs.), nurse
Alford William, blacksmith, West st
Ayre George Thomas, farmer, Lower Queendart
Ayre Michael, farmer, Downe
Ayre Thomas, farmer,Witheridge moor
Baker Charles, dairyman, Litterbarn
Baker William, blacksmith
Bennett Harriet (Miss), shopkeeper, Fore street
Bennett James, shoe maker, Fore st
Besley Henry, farmer, East Piliven
Blackford Henry, miller (water), Bradford mill
Board Thos. farmer, Higher Adworthy
Bodley Thos. carpenter, Pullen's row
Boundy Frederick, farmer, Horestone
Bowden Robt. jobbing grdnr.Gunn hole
Bowden Robt. jun. mason, Gunn hole
Bradford Wm. chimney swpr.Penford
Bucknell Robert, farmer, Westeria ho
Bulled Edmund, wheelwright, The Square
Bulled John, dog trainer
Burnett Ann (Miss), dress ma. West st
Chapple Sarah Jane (Mrs.), farmer, Bythen
Churchill Herbert, baker, West street
Churchill Joseph, saddler

Clark Ephraim, Black Dog P.H
Clotworthy John, builder, Fore street
Conner Wm. tailor & draper, South st
Cox Henry, farmer, Heiffers
Cruwys George, farmer, W. Piliven
Cutcliffe Mrs. farmer & landowner, Coombe & New house
Dart William, farm bailiff to Mrs. Cutcliffe, Cannington & Coombe house
Davey John & William, farmers, Malson & Wilson
Dinner William, blacksmith, Fore st
Dummett Thomas, Angel P.H
Eastman James, police constable
Eastmond Edmund, farmer, Muxeries
Fewings Edmund, farmer, Wheadon
Fox Fowler & Co. bankers (branch) (Herbert John Mansfield, manager), wed. & fri. 11 to 2; draw on Barclay & Co. Limited, London E C
Gill Hedley Thorne, assistant overseer & clerk to Parish Council, Lakelands
Greenslade James, shopkeeper, Fore st
Greenslade Susan (Mrs.), news agent, Rose cottage
Greenslade Wm. shoe ma. Bow court
Gunn Charles, Hare & Hounds P.H
Gunn Charles, wheelwright
Gunn Ellen (Mrs.), nurse, South st
Harris John, farmer, Foxdon
Hill John, farmer, South Grendon
Hodge Hy. mason & shopkpr. North st

Holcombe Claude & Mary (Misses), dress makers
Holcombe William, tailor, Fore street
Holt George Frederick M.R.C.S.Eng., L.R.C.P.Lond. physician & surgeon, Lawn cottage
Hooper Robert, piano tuner, Fore st
Huxtable James, farm bailiff to Mrs. Cutcliffe, New house
Lee Robert, builder, Ebrington's row
Lee William, farmer, South Coombe
Maire Amos, miller (water) & shopkpr
Maire Harriet (Mrs.), dairy.Mitre ho
Manley Wm. butcher, Gunn hole
Mansfield Herbert Jn. grocer & draper
Matthews Harold, farmer, Nth.Coombe
Maunder Frank, butcher, Fore street
Maunder Lloyd, farmer, East Essebern
Norrish Geo. gardener to Mrs.Cutcliffe
Partridge Charles, farmer, Lakelands
Partridge William,shoe ma., Rosemont
Phillips Ann (Mrs.), nurse,The Square
Pickard Ann (Mrs.), tailoress, West st
Pullen George Henry, jun. draper & grocer, Post office
Roberts Thomas, farmer, Newland
Robins George, farmer, Adworthy
Rowcliffe Isaac, farmer, Penford
Selley George, butcher, South street
Selley John, farmer, Hill town
Shelley Percy Wilfred Graham M.R.C.S., L.R.C.P. physician &

Molton Union & Cruwys Morchard district, Tiverton union, Cypress ho
Stone Sidney John, resident sergeant, Police station
Stoneman Richard, miller (water), Drayford mill
Thomas Richard, farmer, Leat
Tolley John, farmer, Hellinghayes
Tolley Wm. insur. agent, Rosemont
Trawin Henry Tapp, wool stapler & drug stores
Tucker George (Mrs.), farmer, Wilson
Tucker William Henry, farmer,Higher Queendart
Tucker Wm. Henry, shoe ma. West st
Venner Robert, thatcher, Drayford
Venner Thomas, thatcher, Godswell
Vicary Charles, farmer, Dart Raffe
Volunteer Battalion (4th) Devonshire Regiment (L Co. Capt. Percy W. G. Shelley; Wm. C. Carter, drill instructor)
Way James, carpenter
Way Mary (Mrs.), dress maker
White Frank, farmer, Fore Down
Whitfield Selina (Mrs.), baker
Witheridge & District (The) Dairy Co. Limited (William Greenslade, sec), dairymen
Wreford William, farmer, Bradford

158

Umberleigh, 1 mile east, in the valley of the Taw, across which there is an old wooden bridge; the North Devon railway has a station here. Umberleigh House is the residence of Major-General Douglas Gaye R.A. Adjoining the Umberleigh mansion house was formerly a chapel dedicated to the Holy Trinity, and endowed as a chantry by Joan, heiress of the Champernownes and wife of Sir Ralph Willington kt. but suppressed in 1547 and dismantled in 1800; only small portions of a wall and an ancient doorway now remain.

Langridgeford is a hamlet 1½ miles west with a Bible Christian chapel.

Sexton, Thomas Harris.

Post Office, Atherington.—Thomas Loosemore, sub-post-master. Letters received from Umberleigh R.S.O. at 6.30 a.m.; dispatched at 6.45 p.m. Postal orders are issued here, but not paid. The nearest money order office is at High Bickington & telegraph office at Umberleigh railway station, 1 mile distant

The Rising Sun, Umberleigh.

Arthur Rev. Wm. Wills M.A. Rectory
Edwards Henry Sanders, Millwood cot
Gaye Major-General Douglas R.A. Umberleigh house

COMMERCIAL.

Andrew Jn. & Son, farmers Umberlgh
Arthur George, farmer, Eastacombe
Bedford John, farmer, Burriott, Barton
Bedford Samuel, farmer, Wooton
Beer George, White Hart P.H
Beer John, nurseryman
Beer John, carpenter
Beer Samuel, fruit dealer
Beer William, carpenter
Brownscombe John, brewer & farmer & assistant overseer & collector of taxes, Eastacombe

Champion John, farmer, Little Weir
Church of England Cottage Homes for Waifs & Strays (Miss Amy Barlow, supt.), Rose cottage
Davis William, fruit dealer
Delbridge Thomas, farmer, Fishley rock
Dockings Henry, farmer, Wan Hills
Down John, farmer, Fisherton
Down John, farmer, Little Hall
Down Wm. farmer, Prospect cottage
Guard George, miller (water) & farmer, Umberleigh
Harding James, farmer, Great Knowle
Harris Thomas, stone mason
Hill Frank, Rising Sun P.H. Umberleigh
Joslin William, farmer, Langridgeford

Joslin Wm. Henry, farmer, Langridge
Lemon William, farmer, Wixland
Loosemore Thos. blacksmith, Post office
Mayne Fredk. shoe maker & farmer
Milton John, farmer, Little Knowle
Norman William, road contractor. Langridgeford
Oatway Richard, farmer, Brimridge
Patt Elizabeth (Mrs.), road contractor, Langridgeford
Page William, market gardener
Sage Fanny (Mrs.), road contractor & farmer, Banherry's farm
Webber Joseph, farmer & market gardener, Chantry
Westcott John, farmer, Higher house
Wonnacott Robert, shopkeeper & farmr

ACKNOWLEDGEMENTS

James and Robin Ravilious for kindly offering to write the introduction to this book. Mr J. Rowe and Mrs Marjorie Snetzler of the North Devon Athenaeum for allowing me access to the Athenaeum Library, and to Marjorie in particular for all her help with information. All the members of the public who, over the years, have donated their photographs and recalled their family histories to add to the Archive. The staff of the Beaford Centre who have had to persuade the public that the Archive was closed temporarily to allow me peace and quiet for 'The Books'. Michael Gullick and Rodney Cooper, two of our Employment Trainees, who have done a great deal of the photographic printing for me. The publishers, David & Charles, for permission to print a short extract from their reprint of *Strong's Industries of North Devon*. Finally, my colleague and friend, Janet Williamson, who has assisted me with the compilations all the way through, sorting through captions, putting photocopies ready for paste-up and turning my incredibly illegible 'scribbles' into neat typescript.

Apologies to all the places I have omitted, especially the large village of Swimbridge; my omissions are due solely to lack of photographs of those places.

BIBLIOGRAPHY

Kelly's Directory of Devon, 1902.
Postcard views of North Devon. Tom Bartlett, 1987.
Views of Old Devon, Tom Bartlett.
Views of Old Devon. Rosemary Anne Lauder, 1982.
Bideford in old picture postcards. Muriel Goaman, 1982.
Bideford Gazette, Silver Jubilee Supplement, May 1935.
Various copies of the *North Devon Journal*.
Aspects of Devon History. R.R. Selman, 1985.
The Local Historian's Encyclopaedia. John Richardson, 1986.
Strong's Industries of North Devon. David and Charles, Reprint, 1971.